DOCTOR BY THE SEA

Dr JOHN H HUGHES
B.E.M. (Mil), B.Sc., M.B. B.Ch., LL.M., PhD., D.R.C.O.G.

John Hughes was born in Commins Coch near Machynlleth and attended Machynlleth County School. Five years in the Army during the Second World War were followed by Medical School in Cardiff. From 1955 until 1986 he served as a G.P. in Aberystwyth.

Retirement meant a new challenge and he returned to college; this time to Cardiff Law School. After graduating in law in 1987, Dr Hughes was appointed an Honorary Lecturer in Medical Law at the University of Wales, Aberystwyth, during which time he obtained his PhD. He is married to a doctor, Elinor, an Edinburgh graduate, and has four children and nine grandchildren.

Dr JOHN H. HUGHES

An Autobiography

DOCTOR BY THE SEA

Cymdeithas Lyfrau Ceredigion Gyf.

Published by Cymdeithas Lyfrau Ceredigion Gyf.
Room B5, The United Theological College, King Street,
Aberystwyth, Ceredigion SY23 2LT.
First published: October 2002
Reprinted October 2002
ISBN 1-902416-71-6
Set in 10.75 on 13.75 pt Adobe Garamond
Printed by Cambrian Printers, Llanbadarn Road, Aberystwyth SY23 3TN
Cover design by Welsh Books Council

Dedicated to my wife for her unselfish support;
also to my children,
and in memory of my parents.

CONTENTS

PREFACE

The healer has long held an honoured place in Welsh society. Those medieval practitioners, the physicians of Myddfai, achieved almost mythical status, and over the centuries 'wizards' of various kinds tended to the ailments of the poor and, indeed, very often the not-so-poor. Public health improved immeasurably in the wrongly despised Victorian Age, when the 'family doctor' became a respected figure in Welsh towns and villages. The author of this absorbing and entertaining autobiography, Dr John H. Hughes, is a fine example of this breed.

Born on a smallholding in Commins Coch, Montgomeryshire, in 1921, he recalls being given a tablespoon of malt and cod liver oil every morning. That will ring bells with those born a decade or so afterwards. The house was lit by oil lamps and candles. The big event of the year was the Sunday school trip to Aberystwyth. That was the start of his life's journey – a journey that took him, during wartime Army service, to Africa, where as a field hygienist (not yet a qualified doctor) he helped to fight outbreaks of malaria and meningitis. 'I ate well,' he recalls, 'because I was given guinea fowls and eggs in every village I visited.' Country people in Cardiganshire have a similar way of expressing their gratitude to the doctor, although the guinea fowl may be absent!

John H. Hughes had the good sense to marry his 'boss' as a young house surgeon in St David's Hospital, Cardiff, 'a Scots girl, very efficient and very pretty', who was Senior House Surgeon there at the time. It was Aberystwyth's good fortune, as well as his own, that he and Elinor went to live there after Dr D.I. Evans, our own family doctor, incidentally, when I was a boy growing up in Trefechan, offered him the post of 'Assistant with a View' in his practice. The 'view' was of a partnership, which in due course Dr Hughes gratefully accepted. 'Aber' seems to me to have been the perfect choice for a man like him, keen not only to minister to his patients as best he could, but also to play a full part in the life of the community.

I won't anticipate Dr Hughes's own story, not least because he tells it so well himself. What I will say is that I am struck not only by his humanity but also by his courage. He has stood steadfastly by what he believes to be right, when a lesser man might have faltered. In particular, his account in Chapter 8 of his stand over the patient's absolute rights to confidentiality makes instructive reading.

John H. Hughes has never been one to speak less than the truth as he sees it, and there is some plain speaking in this book about such matters as repeat prescriptions and the present vogue for counselling. He has something to say too about legal and ethical aspects of modern medicine, as one would expect from a man who after 'retiring' – or 're-tyreing,' as he correctly puts it – had the energy and resolve to study law and become an Honorary Lecturer in Medical Law in Aberystwyth. As if this were not enough, he went on to research for a PhD, his fourth degree from the University of Wales. What an example to us all!

Being a doctor is a serious business, and doctors need a sense of humour. Dr Hughes does not fall short in this department. One of the delights of this book is the examples he provides of what he calls medical humour, all the funnier because it is often unintentional. A laugh a day may not keep the doctor away, but it sure helps your recovery.

I urge everyone to buy this book, so rich in wisdom, common sense and learning.

Herbert Williams
Cardiff

INTRODUCTION

'No-one should write a book unless he has a message to convey.'
Dr William Evans, Tregaron and Harley Street 1895-1988
A Rare Hero, Buddug Owen, Gee 1999

Do I have a message to convey? I have to ask myself as I embark
on this task. There may not be a definite message but the aim is to
place on record the life of a doctor in a university town – the work,
the frustrations, the anxieties and, above all, the friendliness of the
people I was privileged to serve.

The book is a historical record of a period covering about 80
years of the 20th century and relates to life in a rural Welsh village,
to war service, medical school, medical practice, retirement and
the added pleasure of embarking on another academic career in
the study of the law. Law and Medicine are two very old professions - but not the oldest! - and have had great respect for each
other since the days of Hippocrates (460-377 BC) and probably
many centuries before that. At the end of the 20th century these
two professions are closer together than ever due to the unsavoury
increase in medical litigation and the complex ethical implications
of current medical research.

Medical practice is always a full time job but I found the work
immensely satisfying. Although busy, a doctor's life is never dull –
there is a great deal of humour in a medical practice. For the past
50 years I have been collecting examples of such humour and this
book will be interspersed with examples of what I call 'unconscious' humour, which I define as something a person may say
which is perfectly rational to him and hilarious to the listener. For
example:

In the early hours of the morning I sent a patient into hospital as an emergency. He was elderly and had a strangulated femoral hernia. He was deeply shocked and I was worried about him. I went along to the hospital a few hours later and met the surgeon in the corridor.

'How did my patient get on?' I asked.

'The operation went beautifully,' he replied, 'but the patient died.'

It is very important to have a sense of humour. 'Laugh and the world will laugh with you,' said Ella Wheeler Wilcox (1850-1919). I will go so far as to say that a doctor needs a sense of humour to survive in present-day medical practice. The examples of humour in this book come not only from patients but also from colleagues, friends in the wider community, and the medical periodicals and freebie newspapers which inform, amuse and advertise, to their credit, usually in that order.

My thanks to Mrs Gaynor Breese for historical research, Mr William John Davies for permission to publish a summary of his account of John Jones, Frongoch, Mrs Win Davies for help with translation and Mr Terry Bromley, the artist. And special thanks to Mr Herbert Williams for writing the Preface. Finally, last but not least, my thanks to Mr. Dylan Williams and his colleagues in Cymdeithas Lyfrau Ceredigion. I greatly admire their professionalism.

I hope you enjoy reading this volume. You will not always agree with what I say but that should add to the interest of the book.

Dr John H. Hughes
24 North Parade, Aberystwyth 2002

CHAPTER 1

COMMINS COCH

I was born on 14 December 1921 in the village of Commins Coch, Montgomeryshire. It was a home delivery in accordance with the normal pattern at that time. Every district had a nurse/midwife whose salary was paid by the District Nursing Association. The main finance for this service came from local subscriptions, known locally as *hela at y nyrs*. The local doctor, Dr Llywelyn ap Ivan Davies M.C., was in attendance and I understand that I was a forceps delivery. Dr Ivan ap worked single handed, made up his own medicines and ointments, and had a huge rural area to cover. He lived in a neighbouring village, Cemmaes Road, and had two children. Unfortunately one died at the early age of nine from tuberculosis meningitis. This was in 1947, when an outbreak of tuberculosis occurred in the local school. Three pupils died of the disease. The other son, Hywel, became a Consultant Radiologist at Bronglais Hospital, Aberystwyth. Dr Ivan ap served the district with great distinction – a kind, dedicated and hard working doctor. He was always 'on call' and that, in itself, was a heavy commitment. He was a Physician Extraordinary.

Commins Coch is eight miles from Machynlleth on the Newtown Road. The main road, the A470, bisects the village. On one side of the road there is a row of terraced houses built in 1826 and four terraced but larger houses on the other side. One of these houses was a tavern, Y Llew Coch, but this was closed towards the end of the 19th century probably due to the influence of the chapel, of which my grandfather was a deacon. The village had a school, Commins Coch Council School, and a Chapel – Wesleyan

– and in the days of my youth the activities in the village revolved around these two important establishments. I say 'important' because the school prepared the children for the world outside, and the chapel set standards of behaviour which commanded respect for others, discipline and awareness of the environment.

I am greatly indebted to one of my second cousins, Nigel Hughes, who is a historian, for a glimpse of the family tree on my father's side. It appears that the family hailed from the Dylife/Staylittle area of Montgomeryshire, and the more recent descendants came from the Llangurig district. They were all sons of the soil. My grandfather, John Hughes (1862-1929), branched out into business and became a cattle dealer and a general merchant. He and my grandmother, Sarah Hughes (1858-1938), kept the shop cum post-office in Commins Coch and I spent very many days working in the shop. It was mainly a grocery shop plus some clothes for country-folk. Tea and sugar came in huge chests and it was often my job to measure the tea or sugar into one pound or half-pound bags. Tobacco was also sold, the favourite being Ringers Best for the pipe smokers and Woodbine cigarettes for the workers.

Below is an abridged version of the family tree. It will be noted that the Christian name John was handed down from father to son, this being an old custom which tended to cause some confusion! The post-office was established towards the end of the 19th century and my grandfather was probably the first postmaster. The post-office remained in the family until my mother retired in the early 1960's.

My recollection of the 1920's is that practically every man smoked but that women never smoked and would never be seen in a public house. The farmers brought eggs and butter to the shop to exchange for basic groceries.

My mother's family history is rather vague. It appears that the family came from Merionethshire and there is evidence that they were established in Llanbrynmair in 1811. My mother's father, John Morris, was born in 1850 in Hafodyfoel, an upland farm in

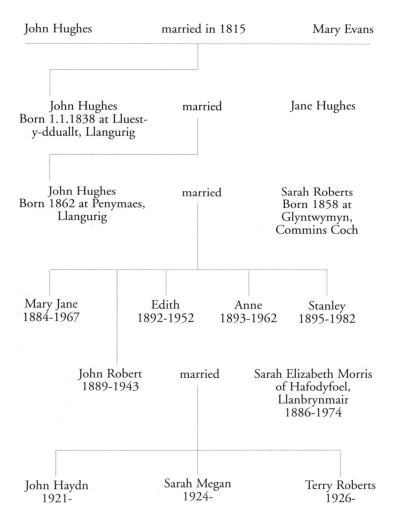

| John Hughes | married in 1815 | Mary Evans |

| John Hughes
Born 1.1.1838 at Lluest-
y-dduallt, Llangurig | married | Jane Hughes |

| John Hughes
Born 1862 at Penymaes,
Llangurig | married | Sarah Roberts
Born 1858 at
Glyntwymyn,
Commins Coch |

| Mary Jane
1884-1967 | Edith
1892-1952 | Anne
1893-1962 | Stanley
1895-1982 |

| John Robert
1889-1943 | married | Sarah Elizabeth Morris
of Hafodyfoel,
Llanbrynmair
1886-1974 |

| John Haydn
1921- | Sarah Megan
1924- | Terry Roberts
1926- |

the parish of Llanbrynmair, about three miles from Commins Coch. He married Sarah Marina Morgan, the daughter of a neighbouring farm called Pantglas. My mother was one of six children. The only son, Evan Morgan Morris, inherited the farm. He was an exceptionally good farmer and his rams won show prizes and commanded a good price when sold. His wife, Catherine, was the kindest of women and an excellent cook. I always remember her rhubarb tarts – unparalleled! The rhubarb grew in the garden, helped by very generous doses of farmyard manure every year.

Of the five daughters, two became nurses, one emigrated to America (which was a common occurrence at that time, especially from Llanbrynmair), one married a postman and settled in Aberystwyth, and my mother on marriage moved to live in Commins Coch. The next generation in Hafodyfoel consisted of two children, John, who became a Veterinary Surgeon, and Meirion, who inherited the farm. One of the great treasures in my memory is that I was able to spend many summers with my cousin on the farm in Hafodyfoel. John was a few years behind me in age and it was he that I had most to do with. It was a pleasure to help with the harvest and to do odd jobs around the farm.

Friday night was a special night – bread making. My aunt used wet yeast, which, I understand, is slower acting than solid yeast. The dough, when mixed, was left in tins placed in a large wooden box near a slow peat fire which lasted until the morning. What a lovely smell met us in the morning. The bread was baked in the typical farmhouse oven of the day. This was in the wall adjoining the fireplace so that the flue from the oven joined the main chimney. The oven would be about 5ft x 3ft, lined with firebricks and with a door 18 inches square. A fire was lit inside the oven using good quality wood, usually oak. After a while, most of the ashes were removed but some were pushed to the sides of the oven. The large bread tins were then put in the oven and, after a suitable interval, were taken out and replaced by a huge fruit cake and smaller cakes. One baking a week was the usual pattern. Very few farmers now bake their own bread – more is the pity.

Two other things about my stay in Hafodyfoel come to mind. On Friday nights we had to take a dose of *wermod lwyd*, which I think was designed to avoid indigestion and help the bowels. The other adventure, which is ingrained in my mind, is that to wash in the morning we went outside to the yard with a bar of red Lifebuoy soap and washed under the *pistyll*. Every farm had a *pistyll* – a small waterfall – about 3 to 4feet high. I have failed to find an English word for *pistyll* but I have a photograph of one from Montgomeryshire and a pen and ink drawing of another in rural Cardiganshire, which is reproduced with the permission of the artist, Mr Terry Bromley. It was, of course, summertime when I was in Hafodyfoel and washing in the nice cold mountain water was the best possible way to wake up.

We got up early on the farm. At about 10.00 a.m. the men, my uncle and the servants, had what was called *bait* – a little food – then back to work. After lunch the master and the servants slept for an hour, except during the hay harvest with rain threatening. The 'nap' after lunch is something which I still practise whenever possible. Fifteen minutes is enough for me – *cysgu a deffro*. Winston Churchill did the same even in wartime. I think this is a good habit to develop especially after a heavy meal. Another good habit is to get up early and don't put your dressing gown on – get dressed! I get up at 6.15 a.m. every day including Sunday. When I was working as a very busy doctor I valued this quiet time. As Angela Rippon's father said many years ago, 'at that time you can enjoy the day before others contaminate it.' Hafodyfoel introduced me to work at an early age and I have been fortunate throughout my life that I have been able to work really hard. Leonardo de Vinci was absolutely right when he said, 'Iron rusts from disuse, stagnant water loses its purity and becomes frozen in cold weather; even so does inactivity sap the vigour of the mind.'

We who can work are indeed fortunate. I remember one of my patients, who had been made redundant, saying, 'I wish I could be able to pay income-tax.' That is another way of putting it! and illustrates the tragedy of lack of work.

My immediate family tree can be seen on the following page. The children are all married. Andrew is an electronics engineer and works for British Aerospace Systems. He is married to a nurse. They have two children and live in Buckland Monachorum (near Plymouth). Kathryn is a doctor and married to a doctor. They have three children and live in Oxford. Duncan is a computer

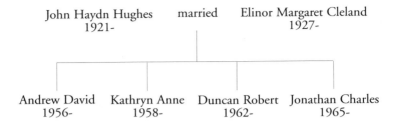

John Haydn Hughes   married   Elinor Margaret Cleland
1921-   1927-

Andrew David   Kathryn Anne   Duncan Robert   Jonathan Charles
1956-   1958-   1962-   1965-

programmer and married to an editor/artist. They have two children and live in San Diego, California. Jonathan is a consultant anaesthetist and married to a nurse. They have two children and live in Cowbridge in the Vale of Glamorgan. To save you adding up, we have nine grandchildren. My wife, Elinor, knits for all of them and remembers their birthdays! The children have all done well due to inheritance of their mother's genes and really excellent tuition in the primary and secondary schools in Aberystwyth. Education must always prepare the child for the wide world outside and must never be too parochial.

In my early days, the pattern of rural village life was very different from the present time. For example, in the period up to the outbreak of war in 1939, the population of the village, including all the farms within the postal district, was approximately 250, with the majority of the men working either on farms, on the railway ('maintenance of the permanent way'), road maintenance, forestry, and some working at nearby slate quarries in Aberangell and Aberllefenni. The usual pattern was for the men to cycle to work on a Monday, stay in 'lodgings', and return on Friday.

Employment was an absolute necessity because there was no formal unemployment benefit at that time. I do not remember anyone in abject poverty, although two families were 'on the parish' (*ar y plwyf*). This form of public assistance had a stigma attached to it but it did provide a minimum sustenance to those in need. It was the forerunner of Social Security, as we know it.

My family lived in a stone house called Tycerrig. My bedroom was adjacent to the stable and our carthorse often kept me awake by stamping its feet. Tycerrig was a smallholding of about 40 acres and had the usual farm buildings. We kept two or three milking cows, an occasional calf, sheep, chickens, a pig and one or two riding ponies. I helped with the milking, gathering of the eggs, cleaning the cowshed (*carthu'r beudy*) and looking after the pig. We did have a manservant but he was mainly involved in my father's work as a cattle dealer. It was, more often than not, my job to milk the cows when I came home from school. The many cats we had would line up in the cowshed and I used to direct the milk from the cow's udder directly into their mouths! My father did not approve of this. We, the children, drank a lot of milk. It was quite common for us to have a hot milk drink at night, containing either Ovaltine, Bengers Food or Bournvita, to mention the names that I can remember.

We had an excellent garden which provided us with all the vegetables we wanted throughout the year. In the autumn the potatoes would be stored in a 'mediaeval tump'. A large hole was dug in one corner of the garden and lined with straw. The potatoes were put in and covered with straw. Finally, all was covered by soil. The potatoes never froze and were readily available by making a small hole at the side of the *tump tatws*. It has been said that an inch of straw is better than twelve inches of soil for insulation. (The Aertex vest is based on a similar principle.) Every house in the village had its garden, and the annual horticultural shows held in Llanbrynmair and the surrounding villages invariably had exhibits from Commins Coch. It was customary to visit one or other of the really good gardens after chapel on a Sunday morning. The produce from the gardens played a significant part in the nutrition of the people at that time. When the war came in 1939 the 'Dig for Victory' campaign was already operative! The gardens produced not only potatoes, but cabbage, carrots, swedes, onions, radishes, beetroot, beans, lettuce, vegetable marrow, and the customary herbs of sage and mint – all organically grown! A boiled onion was commonly eaten, with added pepper and butter. It is now recognised that onions, garlic and leeks can lower the cholesterol in the blood. The boiled onion was obviously an example of healthy eating and we would do well to return to it. In the first half of the 20th century many of the rural villages in Mid-Wales were visited by *Sioni Winwns*, a Breton on his bicycle who wore a black beret and spoke Welsh. His bicycle was laden with strings of onions and he had a ready sale for his product. It is interesting to note, in retrospect, that as a nation we were healthier during the war than at any other time. Food was rationed: butter 2 ozs, sugar ½ lb, cooking fat 2 ozs, margarine 2 ozs – all per week. The bread was the National Loaf, mainly brown. There is no doubt that today we are eating too much. I used to suggest to my patients who were overweight to say after a meal, 'I could eat more,' rather than having to say, 'Oh dear, I've eaten too much.'

What else did we eat in those days? I can say at once that we were mainly self-sufficient. On our small farm we had milk in plenty, cream, fresh eggs, farm butter and buttermilk (*llaeth enwyn*) to drink. The buttermilk came from another farm. My mother made jam from the fruit bushes in the garden – black currants, gooseberries, red currants, rhubarb – and blackberries from the hedgerows. Plums and apples were plentiful and in most years we had cherries from a huge tree in one of our fields. We had a 'boiling hen' from time to time. The pig was killed when about 18 months old and this gave us home cured ham and bacon which would last us for about a year. We ate every bit of the pig, even the brain. Nothing was ever wasted. I did not stay at home on the day that the pig was killed. This was done by a man from a neighbouring village who killed the pig by cutting its throat with a very sharp knife. The poor pig screamed for a short time but it felt more like half an hour. Very cruel – once heard never forgotten.

I can't remember my mother making butter. We bought our butter from a nearby farm and I understand that the supply continued throughout the war! Bread was also bought although we did have an 'oven in the wall'. Tycerrig was completely refurbished in 1998-99 and the picture in the plate section shows the position of the oven – on the right of the fireplace.

Porridge was a basic breakfast item served with pure cream and invariably followed by bacon and eggs with *toast yn y badell* – bread fried in the fat that cooked the bacon. Beef dripping was stored in earthenware pots and we spread this on our bread. This was long before the days of concern about cholesterol! There was the belief that you had to have a good breakfast before going to work or school. Sometimes for breakfast we had *llymru* – called *bwdran* in Cardiganshire. This was made from oatmeal which was allowed to soak overnight in cold water, strained in the morning and cooked in a saucepan. Many people did not like it because it was a little sour, but I liked it. The only breakfast cereals that I remember were 'Force' and 'Grape Nuts'.

We ate a lot of rabbits, the occasional hare, pheasants, wood pigeons and trout. Our farm border for about one mile was the river Twymyn, a tributary of the River Dovey. I spent a lot of time fishing using a worm as bait. Fly-fishing was not a practical proposition because of the overhanging trees along most of the river-bank. The best time for worm fishing was when the river was in flood. Finding worms was sometimes a problem – the best ones came from underneath a partly dried cow pat. We had to buy a licence to fish and the season extended from March to September.

The name of the river is interesting. It is called Twymyn, which is the Welsh word for 'fever.' The river originates in Dylife, runs from there to Llanbrynmair, then on to Commins Coch, and joins the Dovey in Cemmaes Road. Dylife was at one time a major lead mining area. The lead sulphite waste produced after smelting found its way into the river and killed the fish – hence the name 'Fever.' The lead mining industry declined and gradually disappeared, and the fish came back to the river. If I went fishing in the morning when the river was in flood I could guarantee a plateful of trout for lunch. Fresh trout curl up in the frying pan! The salmon came up river from the Dovey and, when the water was clear, a friend of mine was an expert at getting the occasional salmon out of the water using a rabbit snare around its tail. A strictly illegal procedure!

My recollection of the early days is that we were well fed. My mother was an excellent cook and she produced gorgeous tarts cooked in an oil stove. We also had an oven that was part of a Triplex grate but it was the oil stove that cooked the meat and cakes.

All country folk coped with minor illnesses and rarely involved the doctor. My mother made elderberry syrup. This was a concentrated extract of elderberry fruit and we had to take it in hot water plus an Aspro when we had a cold. Another cold remedy was to drink *dŵr oddi-ar jam cyrens duon* – this was hot water with a good dollop of homemade blackcurrant jam. We liked this and it probably contained a certain amount of Vitamin C (cf Ribena today). Another common medication in the villages was to take a foul tasting mixture – one teaspoonful of Tinct. Rhei. Co with one teaspoonful of Sp. Aether Nit. in hot water, again with the customary Aspro (Aspirin). There is no doubt that Spirit Aether Nitrate was a drug of addiction and people used to buy it regularly 'just in case' they had a cold – or so they said! My mother had great faith in Thermogene and we had this applied to our chests when we had a cold, where it was left in position for about three days. Sometimes red flannel was used instead. One practice which I particularly remember was that we, the children, had to take a tablespoonful of malt and cod liver oil every morning. This was a common occurrence in Mid-Wales at the time. Occasionally we had to take 'Parish's Food' – a foul tasting iron medicine. This prophylactic medication may well have saved us from tuberculosis which was rife at that time. We had only our immune system to keep that dreaded disease at bay.

In common with the majority of the villagers we only had 'butcher meat' (*cig ffresh*) on Sundays. This was delivered by 'Johnny Post' whose son was a butcher in Borth and whose father delivered the meat on Saturday on his bicycle. Sunday was a day for chapel with two services and the Sunday school. Sunday tea was a special treat as we had tinned Californian Pears and Peaches. I well remember the picture of the growing area on the tin, and much later in life I saw from a bus the fruit-growing farms in California, which brought back happy memories of the 'fruit and cream'.

My two sisters, Megan and Terry, had a reasonably sheltered upbringing. The three of us got to the County School. This was in Machynlleth and getting there was an adventure in itself. We had to cycle to Cemmaes Road (2½ miles) then catch a bus to Machynlleth (6 miles). The weather was often inclement and we had yellow oilskin capes for protection against the rain. I recollect that in my early days in the County School I had to take my lunch with me and I seem to remember that my parents had to pay for the books and tuition. Mr Meyler was the Headmaster during my first year and he was followed by Mr Haddon Roberts – probably one of the best headmasters in Wales at that time. He was a strict disciplinarian and the pupils who wanted to work were encouraged in every way. I owe a great deal to him because, looking back, I was obviously a 'late achiever' and needed to be pushed. The other teacher I remember was Mr W.B. Jones, the English master. He enabled me to understand and enjoy Shakespeare. Very many times I have quoted Macbeth to my patients who could not sleep because of emotional problems. Shakespeare's majestic description of sleep is so perfect:

> Sleep that knits up the ravell'd sleave of care,
> The death of each day's life, sore labour's bath,
> Balm of hurt minds, great nature's second course.
>
> Macbeth Act II Scene II 36

Julius Caesar was another Shakespearian favourite and in my later capacity as a Clinical Assistant in Obstetrics the name Caesar had a special significance! I left school in 1939 and my school certificate had two distinctions: Chemistry (taught by Mr Haddon Roberts) and English Literature (taught by Mr W.B. Jones). Good teachers are so valuable and it is often very many years afterwards before this fact is recognised and appreciated.

As already mentioned, my two sisters gained admission to the County School and the three of us had to do our homework on four nights of the week. Friday night was free and in the winter our major hobby was rug making. The wool was not 'ready-cut' in those days – we had to cut it ourselves. We made many rugs and some are in use in my house today or by the beds of our grandchildren. I made two rugs after retirement and they are shown in the photographs in the plate section.

In the later years in school we had a car and we were able to use this for school when my father did not want it. I passed my driving test soon after my 17th birthday, having practised driving 'off the road' for months before my birthday. My two sisters branched out into the world. Megan became a nurse and Terry went to the University in Aberystwyth to study bacteriology in the context of Dairying. She was subsequently employed as a dairy bacteriologist in Wem, Dolgellau and Newport (Mon.).

My mother insisted that I had music lessons. This meant going on my bicycle to Cemmaes (about four miles away). I hated this. 'Practising' was mandatory for one hour every day. I placed a clock on the piano to make sure that I did not exceed the time. In retrospect it was a complete waste of time trying to teach me to play the piano. I do not understand music at all; I can't sing but do enjoy listening to *Dechrau Canu Dechrau Canmol,* the Welsh equivalent of Sunday Half Hour on the television, and to Classic FM on the radio. I can listen to the radio and do something else at the same time – too often nowadays this means falling off to sleep! My sister, Megan, became an accomplished pianist and to this day plays the organ/piano in her local chapel. My father had no knowledge or interest in music and I followed him. My mother was very musical and came from a musical family. That particular gene did not come my way, but I am very pleased to say that all my children are musical. Andrew plays the piano, oboe and saxophone; Kathryn the viola; Duncan the clarinet; Jonathan the flute. My wife, Elinor, is the musical brain in our family and is in constant touch with music through playing the bassoon in Philomusica, Windband, and in smaller 'house visiting groups' very similar to the old days when four or five people came to our house in Commins Coch just to sing. The lesson is clear. If you are given a talent – use it. If the talent is not there you can't buy it in Woolworth's or any other shop. Try something else!

To go back in time to life in a rural village. We did not have electricity – our mode of light was a large hanging oil lamp in our front room (*gegin ore*) later replaced by an Aladdin lamp. Both lamps heated the room. Upstairs and around the house we had candles. Hot water bottles were the earthenware type with a central opening. The water was still warm in the morning and this is what we used for morning ablutions.

There was no television but we did have a 'wireless'. This was attached to an outdoor aerial and an 'earth'. Two batteries, a dry battery and a wet battery, powered it. The wet battery had to be recharged quite often and, fortunately, a local farmer was able to charge the batteries for the village. I remember the great excitement of hearing the Welsh language on the wireless for the first time.

My mother had a hard time. Like all other housewives in those days she was a second-class citizen. The status of women in society had not changed since biblical times, as described in Exodus 20.17 where a man's wife is listed with such items as his slave, his donkey, and his ox. She was a chattel, a movable possession. The man was always the boss.

In addition to her household duties the housewife on a farm had to feed the hens, collect the eggs, feed the calves, and help with the hay harvest in the summer. My mother did not have to work in the fields because we had plenty of men around. Villagers came to help and were given ham, bacon or potatoes in return. Monday was washing day and it was sometimes difficult to get the fire going under the huge boiler. Washing the clothes was hard work – the soaking, the scrubbing, the boiling, the mangling and the drying. Then came the ironing after liberal application of 'Robin Starch'. Ironing was by a 'box' iron which contained red-hot inserts taken from the centre of the fire. Women took pride in the whiteness of their washing on the clothes line. Clothes were not put out to dry on a Sunday. The clothes were always carefully 'aired' because of a belief that damp clothes caused rheumatism. Not true.

The men workers wore sacks when having to work in the rain – a sack over the shoulder held in position by a six-inch nail, and another sack around the waist held together by string. The sacks used for weather protection were much better made and thicker than the ones we see now. Women often wore a *ffedog* (apron) made from flour bags, again good strong material. Spring-cleaning was an annual ritual. Everything, and I mean everything, was moved, washed or cleaned and polished. I well remember the smell of *cwyr* (wax) *a turpentine*. The women got very tired at this time of the year and often became depressed. There is a reference to this seasonal ailment in the Bible, and it occurs also in the autumn when the leaves are falling – *Cwympiad y dail.* Doctors recognise something similar and call it 'seasonal affective disorder'. This is related to a lack of light and sunshine and appears in the autumn. It has nothing to do with spring-cleaning.

I spent most of my free time on the farm. We always had a pony and I used to enjoy riding that. My father insisted that I had to ride without a saddle because of the danger of one's foot being caught in the stirrup if one should fall from the horse. This had happened to him and he was permanently lame. My friend in the village was Richard Robert Lumley and he was often on the farm with me. I looked after the pig and kept the pigsty clean. Richard Robert and I cut bracken (*rhedyn*) as bedding material for the pig. We also cut a lot of firewood, especially morning sticks because you could not get a morning cup of tea until a fire had been lit. This was before the days of Calor gas and the Aga! We both helped my father move thousands of sheep to Cemmaes Road station for trucking by train to the Midlands. My father was a cattle dealer but in the main he bought sheep and he did this by visiting farms. The cattle he bought were mainly sold in the market in Welshpool on a Monday and/or Oswestry on a Wednesday.

To earn a little money Richard Robert and I gathered moss that grew on the mountainous common land, and this had a ready sale at six (old) pence a bag. I also caught moles, skinned them, salted and dried the skins and sold them. The money came in useful for our annual outing, the Sunday school trip to Aberystwyth. That was a great event and the climax of the day was a visit to Woolworth's! The maximum cost of any items sold was six pennies. The main railway line (Great Western Railway) ran in front of our house and we had a 'HALT' where most of the trains stopped. In the old days you could tell the time by the trains because they were so punctual. The HALT has long disappeared and there are now no stopping trains between Caersws and Machynlleth.

My father's only brother, Stanley, was also a dealer – mainly of pigs. He became 'Lord of the Manor' during the war when he bought all the fields and small farms that were on the market at that time. He was a very good businessman and very much an entrepreneur – selling seeds to the farmers and horse racing with considerable success. He was a producer of electricity (direct current) for the village, and a Home Guard leader during the war. He became an Alderman of the County Council and fought hard for the rights of the common man.

When my paternal grandmother died in 1938 my uncle Stanley inherited the property. My father had already inherited the farm where we lived when his father died. My parents decided to build a modern semi-bungalow on one of our fields with a small shop to accommodate the village post office. In this new house we were blessed with water on tap from our own supply and a bathroom with plenty of hot water from a back boiler in the kitchen grate. It was nice and civilised to have a modern toilet instead of the 'privy' in the garden which we had in Tycerrig. Prior to that we had a 'two-holer' with *Y Cymro* cut up into appropriate pieces as toilet paper. If only the Editor knew what became of his paper!

Water was a problem in the village. The only source was a waterspout from a spring and the water was collected in buckets. In a really hot summer the water dried up and the villagers had a journey of about half a mile to another source (*pistyll oer*) which never dried up. It was after the war that a mains supply of water came to the village. At the inauguration of the new supply, it was said that having the new system was as important as man landing on the moon. It certainly was more relevant to the people of Commins Coch.

When we moved to our new house we let Tycerrig to a tenant farmer and ultimately the farm was sold to subsequent tenants, Mr and Mrs T. Lewis. The transfer of the village post office to our new house was a blessing in disguise because my father died at the age of 54 from cancer of the stomach. I was in the Army at the time and the post office was a source of income for my mother and a meeting place which kept her in daily contact with people. She gradually added other things to sell in the shop and at the time of her retirement she had quite a good grocery business selling a little of almost everything – including casks of Somerset cider for the farmers at harvest time. She also sold newspapers; the two favourites being the *Liverpool Daily Post* and the *Daily Mail*, with the *County Times* and *Y Cymro* on Saturdays.

The local postman, D.E.Corfield, was a great character and I am pleased to say that I interviewed him on tape in 1972 when he was 84 and long retired. He lost one arm in an accident when he was working in a quarry but he was able to do almost everything with his one arm. I recollect that his pocket watch had just one hand – the hour hand – but that did not worry Corfield, as he was affectionately called, he could tell the time to the exact minute. He was a part-time walking postman and his route covered 11½ miles which he did every day without illness for 30 years. I acted as a 'locum' for him when he had his two weeks holiday in August and I was an impoverished medical student at the time. The post was delivered even on Christmas day and Corfield had to carry the parcels and letters in his

Stoneware hot water bottle.

big post-bag. He used to curse the very small parcels which were difficult to locate in his big bag!

One unique feature of rural life was that we had a travelling dentist. He was the well known T. E. Nicholas who lived in Aberystwyth and called in specific houses in mid-Wales once every other week. Our house was one of his 'surgeries' and all my mother had to do was to put a chair outside the back door with a bucket and a glass of water. 'Niclas', as he was called, confined his dental work when on tour to extractions only. For false teeth etc. the patients had to go to his surgery in Aberystwyth. Niclas was not a qualified dentist but his name got on to the Dental Register automatically when that was established in 1921. He was formerly a minister of religion but was too outspoken for that profession. His wife was a qualified dentist and she was the one who taught him dentistry. He was very much an outspoken communist and his articles in *Y Cymro* in 1938/39 were politically inflammatory. When war came in 1939 he was detained under the Emergency Regulations and spent some time in prison. When in prison he wrote, on toilet paper, poetry which was later published in book form as *Canu'r Carchar* [Poetry from Prison], Gwasg Gomer 1942). Despite his politics he was a very clever and exceptionally nice man.

Welsh was the language of the village and the Dovey valley had its own dialect. This characteristic dialect extended to Dovey Junction to the south, close to Aberdovey and Dinas Mawddwy to the North and as far as Carno to the east. A lady living in the Machynlleth area wrote a series of articles in the local community paper *Blewyn Glas* under the pseudonym Corrisa Jôs. She wrote in the vernacular which brings out the local dialect. Some of the articles were later published and I am most grateful to the Editor of the book *Ysgrife'r Randibw* for permission to reproduce one extract, taken at random, of this very clever exposition of the local dialect. The content of the article is not important. I suggest that the reader asks a friend to read this out aloud and thereby hear the local dialect as very cleverly expressed in this quote from the book:

Ond deud oeddwn i am ddydd Sadwrn dwetha. Oedd tre
Machynlleth, wrs gwrs, fel pentre yng nghefen gwlêd
Eisland: plant yn whare slej ar Strît Maengwyn; tractors
ffarmwrs wedi'i parcio ymhobman yn giythgiam o anniben
(oedd yr ielo leins, wrs gwrs, o'r golwg dan eira; efri clowd,
fel Jac y Sais, has a silfyr leining); pobol yn cerdded yng
nghianol y ffordd; Bryn y twrne efo sached o fwyd i'r babi
newydd yn scêtio heibio Cloc y Towar; a Freda Henllan yn
iste mewn bocs tractor wth Siop Jips. Dein giato pawb, mi
oedd pethe'n gomon! Ac i goroni'r cwbwl dyma glompen o
helicoptar yn fflio i fyny'r strît, yn neud un tro teidi yn
rawyr ac yn landio'n ddeche reit yn union o flaen ty Edwart
Pughe. Mi redodd Darona a finne i fyny cyn gynted ag y
gallen ni – dydi'n coese ni ddim fel y buo nhw, mwya'r piti
– i weld be oedd yr ecseitment. Oedd Darona'n meddwl me
imyrjensi milc dilifri i gogie Top Shop oedd o, ond oeddwn
i'n credu'n siwr me Aelwyn o Ddrwen oedd yn galw i weld
i dêd ar i ffordd i'r dre. Ffordd doech chi o Drwen ar y
ffasiwn dywydd, yntê, ond efo helicoptar? Ffor bynnag,
oedd na dwr go lew o bobol yn watsied yr halibalw. Arwel
Peleg yn trio cyfansoddi ciên i 'Helicoptars Bêch y Wlêd' ar
gyfer i record nesa, a Iorwerth Hughes yn wondro tybed
fydde'r Cownsil yn barod i byrnu helicoptar at iws y Maer.
Un ned oedd o *ddim* yno oedd Ifan Llwyngronfa. I me'n
rhaid i bod hi'n giythgiam o luwchie yn Melinbarhedyn
yna cyn y colle Ifan show fel hon.

Mi êth yn nos ddudew amser landiodd yr helicoptar.
Oedd i hen freichie hi yn neud y ffasiwn wynt oedd yr
eira'n whythu i bob man ac yn twllu'r strît. Ond pan
oleuodd hi, dyma rwy ffwdan o gyfeiriad yr Hosbitol fêch,
a Doctor Jones yn arwen y ddynes fêch yna o'r Waen i
mewn i'r helicoptar. Y griadures fêch yn disgwyl twins, nen
diwc, a wedi dod i lawr i Hosbitol dre ar dractor, ac wan yn
goffod mynd i Aberystwyth ar hêst. Dein giato pawb! Y
pethe den ni, ferched, yn mynd trwyddyn nhw. Fel dedes i

wth Darona: i me hi'n ddê ned dynion sy'n ciêl babis. 'Pe base hyn yn digwydd i John,' meddwn i, 'mi neuse gyment o ffys mi fydde'n rhaid ciêl sgwadron o'r Red Arros o leia i'w gario fo i Ben-glais, a mi fydde'n hewian fod y rheini'n slô!'

Ysgrife'r Randibŵ, Corrisa Jones, Y Lolfa 1983

No account of the village would be complete without a reference to a man who lived before his time. His name was John Jones and he lived in a farm called Frongoch situated at the foot of Moel Eiddew (453m). He was a great reader of engineering journals and taught himself to make all manner of mechanical gadgets. An account of this man's remarkable achievements has been produced by his manservant, William John Davies, and I am greatly indebted to my friend William John for permission to include extracts from his excellent article which was published in the local community newspaper *Blewyn Glas* in June 1997.

The farm was a family owned one, as opposed to the other farms in the area at the beginning of the 20th century, which were 'estate' farms. John Jones admitted that he was not much of a farmer – his main interests were reading and applying what he read to making mechanical items on the farm. His father did not share his interest and gave no support. His mother, however, paid for the technological books that he needed. At the age of 14 he made a gramophone having bought basic parts and making the other bits and pieces. It worked well. His next venture was to produce electricity. This he achieved by buying and adapting a new turbine (Pelton Wheel). There was always plenty of water in Frongoch and this was channelled and directed to the wheel, which operated a dynamo. He then wired his house and buildings and was the first in the area to have electricity. Later he made his own wireless which worked well for many years, and it was he who charged the 'wet batteries' for the villagers. There is no doubt that John Jones had a scientific mind. He was constantly thinking of new and more efficient ways of approaching something which had gone on without change for centuries. Hence he constructed well-drained roads, and rebuilt a damaged car which he used extensively after converting it to a small lorry.

When war came farmers had to produce their own animal food because food for animals could not be imported. John Jones took advantage of the free advice available from agricultural experts. He was the first in the district to cultivate 'Marrow Stem Kale' which his cows liked and, as a result, they produced as much milk in the winter as in the summer. Silage was also introduced at this time and John Jones treated his hay in this way. The cattle thrived on this. Frongoch butter was in great demand, even during the war!

His extensive reading of agricultural journals led him to a new method of re-seeding his fields using specific grass seeds – usually Aberystwyth S.25 rye grass. He bought his first tractor in 1935, a second hand Fordson to replace the horse which, he claimed, had to be fed every day and did very little work. There is a lot more one could say about John Jones but this brief summary of the article by William John Davies gives an insight into the life of this gifted man. He died in his 90th year and there is no doubt that he lived before his time. I must again pay tribute to William John Davies for writing this article, in immaculate Welsh, which will remain as a valuable contribution to the history of Mid-Wales.

CHAPTER 2

THE CHAPEL

The chapel was the centre of village activity. It was a branch of the Welsh Wesleyan faith. There is an account in *Yr Eurgrawn Wesleyaidd,* 1869, of the missionary work in the district, which started in 1803 when preachers came to the village to conduct services in certain houses – Cwmbychan Mawr, Pandy, and Tycerrig (my old home). The congregation increased and the local 'school room' was used for formal services. This soon became too small and a proper chapel was built which opened on 9 April 1809. As time went on, the chapel fabric deteriorated and the chapel itself became too small for the congregation. It was decided to build a new and bigger chapel and this was opened on 20 May 1868. It was described as 'a lovely chapel, well constructed inside and out and on the best situation in the village. It can seat 200 comfortably.'

The list of contributors to the building of the chapel includes the names of the occupants of the Red Lion, which proves that there was a tavern in the village at that time. The chapel was again repaired and renovated in 1925 – see the picture in the plate section. The chapel is still there but there has been a steady decline in membership over the past 25 years and in recent years there has been only one Sunday service with no resident minister and no Sunday School. On Sunday 26 November 2000 the chapel closed for the winter. Will it reopen? I doubt it.

In my early days there were morning and evening services with a Sunday School during the afternoon. We learned a lot in the Sunday School. I clearly remember the excellent teacher I had,

Elias Humphreys, a man who lived before his time. He had a map of Palestine which he regularly referred to. Many years later I was travelling by bus from Jerusalem to the Sea of Galilee, and as I looked out through the window I could swear that I had been there before. This was because Elias Humphreys had been able to convey the image of Israel, although he himself had never been there. It is a shame that he did not have the opportunity to visit the land which he knew so well in his mind. The Sea of Galilee was calm on the day that I went by boat from Tiberias to Capernaum but I remember that Elias Humphreys knew about the sudden storms that could 'churn' that inland sea.

On the Sea of Galilee small boats run 'trips in the bay' from Tiberias. Two Tregaron farmers were on holiday. They wanted to go for a boat trip and asked the owner of the boat,

'How much is the trip?'

'£5 each for half an hour,' he replied.

'Too much,' said one of the Tregaron men. 'Far too much. No wonder Jesus Christ walked!'

The testaments we used in Sunday School were half English and half Welsh. Welsh was the language of the chapel and the village. Elias Humphreys taught us to refer to the English version as well as the Welsh. This was a valuable contribution to bilingual education!

Through the Sunday School we, the children, collected money for the Foreign Mission (*Y Gymdeithas Dramor*) and the majority of us were presented annually with a book as a prize. Many years later, when in West Africa during the war, I was able to admire and appreciate the work done by the missionaries – not only preaching but also operating schools and health clinics alongside places of worship. It was nice to know that the pennies we collected were put to good use.

Our new bungalow in Commins Coch was next door to Wesley Villa where the Minister and his family lived. We became very friendly with all the ministers' children that came and went every third year, as was customary on the Wesleyan circuit. We had outstanding ministers, notably James Elder, G. Lloyd Brookes, John Henry Griffiths and Gwilym Tilsley (who later became Archdruid of Wales). One minister, Rev Idris Davies, had tuberculosis and died after prolonged hospitalisation. Tuberculosis was the dreaded disease in the early and middle years of the 20th century and I will refer briefly to it in another chapter.

The services in the chapel were very well attended in the pre-war years. I used to look forward to the annual *Cyfarfod Diolchgarwch*, the Thanksgiving Service, when the Minister would talk about things we country folk understood – the soil, the seed, the ploughing, the crops, the harvest, and what is now called the environment and its preservation. Another major event was the *Cyfarfod Mawr*, the special preaching meeting when a 'top line' preacher would be invited. The chapel would be full to overflowing. For the evening meeting three ministers would take part. A junior minister would read the scripture, a more senior minister would pray, and then the big man himself ascended to the pulpit. It was clearly understood that he would have to preach for at least an hour, otherwise the chapel would not be having value for money! The singing was always outstanding and it was great to hear them preaching in the *hwyl*. It is difficult to convey in English what is meant by *yr hwyl* – the preacher would raise his voice, a gentle rise and fall, half singing, and in this way emphasize some particular point which the audience could not fail to remember.

There is a story about this method of preaching which has an element of unconscious humour. A minister was referring to the gift of water as, 'Hydrogen and Oxygen coming together to give us water. Free [as it was at that time].'

'Friends,' he said, with both arms outstretched. 'If I had hydrogen in my left hand and oxygen in my right hand, I could make water in this pulpit!'

Rural chapels were always dependent on lay preachers and some of them were very good indeed. One of the best that I remember was a Mr Disley from Aberangell. You could listen to every word he said, the real test of a good sermon.

We also had meetings during the week and I vaguely remember signing the 'Pledge' in the Band of Hope but I doubt whether I knew what it meant at the time. It probably had some unconscious effect on me. One of the most enjoyable aspects of going to chapel was the meeting of friends outside the chapel after the morning service, when we had a chat about everything and nothing. We might visit a garden. There were some very good ones quite near the chapel. A not uncommon habit after the evening service in the summer was to *hebrwng* people home – this meant going half way with those who lived some distance away.

A 'watchnight' service was often held in the chapel on the last night of the year. It was more of a concert than a service and we all left after midnight to enter a new year with renewed faith and goodwill. I think the word 'goodwill' sums up the influence of the chapel – goodwill towards all men, with absolute respect for the minister, the teachers, the doctor, the policeman and, to a lesser extent, the elders of the chapel. Goodwill towards others demands discipline, self-discipline and discipline in the home. We respected our parents. Any unruly behaviour would make my mother look towards the birch-rod. Every house had a birch-rod. It did no harm at all despite what the do-gooders say today and in this I stick to the verse in Proverbs 29.15: 'The rod and reproof give wisdom; but a child left to himself bringeth his mother to shame.'

On New Year's Day we, the children, went around the houses singing outside the door and expecting a New Year gift (*calennig*) – this meant a penny here and there. People could not afford more, and half-a-penny would buy a quarter pound of sweets. Sunday in the country was always a day of rest and chapel going. Even on a hot sunny Sunday the hay, if ready, would not be harvested. This 'rule' was broken in the early years of the war because of the need for full-scale food production.

Marriages were solemnized in the chapel. As the bride left her home for the chapel, one or two of the locals would shoot into the air using a double-barrelled gun. When the couple came out of the chapel and entered the bridal car, the children of the village held a rope across the road and the car could not proceed until some money was thrown out of the window. The bridegroom had to pay up! One sad custom made me feel very sorry for the recipient. If a woman had been courting a man, and this man married another woman, the jilted lady would be sent a *ffon wen* by post on the day of the wedding. This was a short white stick with a label attached but no letter and no name of sender. It was looked upon as a joke but it must have hurt the individual concerned.

Funerals were big events and a meeting of the clan. They followed a pattern. The body of the deceased would be brought downstairs and laid in a coffin in the parlour. The coffin was left open and friends would call to see the body and bring a gift to the bereaved family – eggs, butter, ham, cakes, etc. On the funeral day the order of events would be as follows:

Cau at 12.30 pm (putting the lid on the coffin).
Service for the family in the house at 12.45 pm.
Codi at 1.00 pm (the coffin leaves the house for
a public or private service in the chapel, usually public).

The burial was in a parish cemetery, usually two miles away in the village of Darowen. My parents are buried there together with my extended family going back to the beginning of the 20th century and earlier. After the burial, and the customary singing of *O fryniau Caersalem*, it was the usual practice to go to the Darowen schoolroom for the funeral tea. That was a great event!

Darowen is a small village about two miles from Commins Coch. The parish church, dedicated to St Tudur, dates from the 7th century. The present church is said to be the fourth on the same site and was built in 1862. I am pleased to record that the Church is kept going by my cousins and their families, who make up the Pughe family of Cwmbychan Mawr. My late uncle, John Jones Pughe, married my father's sister, Sarah Matilda Hughes. They had fourteen children and unfortunately my aunt died soon after the birth of the last child at the early age of 42. The children were brought up by the girls in the family, mainly by Anora, one of the older children. She was a wonderful 'mother' and a really excellent cook. The Pughe sons settled in farms of their own in the immediate locality. They work very hard and enjoy it. Their farms are a model of perfection and I am very proud and honoured to be part of the family.

There is a historical item which relates to Darowen church. Someone with a lot of money and a lot of compassion decided that the vicars of small isolated churches should be well-read and he presented a set of classical books to, I am told, every rural church in Montgomeryshire. The books given to Darowen church were taken to the College of Librarianship in Aberystwyth and presumably are on display there.

The chapels and rural churches are now in decline. Very few have a resident minister/vicar and many places of worship are being closed because of falling membership and the expense of maintaining the fabric of the buildings. Rural depopulation and the arrival of non-Welsh speaking people to the area has contributed to the decline.

There is a story relating to the influx of our English friends which I am told is true. A deacon called upon an Englishman who had moved into the area inviting him to come to the chapel on Sundays. 'There is no point', said the man. 'It's all Welsh and I won't understand it.'

'That is true,' answered the deacon, 'but the collection is in English!'

I very much welcome the influx of non-Welsh speaking friends to our villages because without them our villages and isolated cottages would be completely deserted, and the vast majority of the newcomers are sympathetic to the needs of the local people and to the environment.

We are fast becoming a secular generation and yet Christian principles are high on our list of priorities. The response of the British public to an appeal to help flood victims in Mozambique was £5million promised in three days, and this increased to £16million by the end of one week. This was in the year 2000.

The world has become our parish and our concern for others has been heightened by television and, more recently, by access to the Internet. We who were born in the first half of the 20th century will have happy memories of the chapel and, in particular, the Sunday school. It made us aware of the world outside our little village and encouraged us to believe that 'Whatsoever thy hand findeth to do, do it with all thy might.' (Ecclesiastes. 9. 10)

CHAPTER 3

THE SCHOOL

Next in importance in the village came the school. I must admit that I have little memory of my time in Commins Coch School. In fact, it is a complete blank. Many years ago I was fortunate enough to have access to the logbook of the school – a most informative record of great historical interest. The Headmaster was obliged to keep a daily record of attendances and any relevant items directly connected with the school and its environment.

The school opened on 24 May 1897 with 36 scholars and a Mr Green as Headmaster. Times were hard. The headmaster repeatedly referred to the difficulty of getting a supply of coal for the school, the difficulty of getting the roof repaired after a storm, and the constant fight against parents who kept their children home from school.

Note the date: 1897. What happened before then? There must have been some teaching going on. There is evidence that some basic teaching was taking place in private houses, and later in a 'school hall'. I referred in Chapter 2 to the use of this room for religious services and this was 90 years at least before the village school was established. There were also Church schools and the nearest to Commins Coch was in Darowen, two miles away, which opened in 1841. A 'board' school opened in Llanbrynmair 2½ miles away on 4 September 1874. Apparently there was some sort of teaching in Llanbrynmair from 1795, but there is no record of Commins Coch children attending this school.

The school in Commins Coch was a direct result of The Elementary Education Act of 1870 which established the principle of public elementary schools. There was concern at the growth of religious indoctrination in the Church schools, and this is why every district, i.e. a parish or municipal borough, had a state aided school built, managed by a 'board' and supervised by inspectors. Section 14 of the above Act states: 'no religious catechism or religious formulary which is distinctive of any particular denomination shall be taught in the school.'

This brought to an end the monopoly of the Church in education and the role of religious instruction was made clear by the law. Section 7 (2) of the Act states: 'any religious observance . . . or instruction in religious subjects . . . shall be either at the beginning . . . or at the end of the [school] meeting.'

In 1876 The Elementary Education Act was passed, which made elementary education compulsory:

> It shall be the duty of the parent of every child to cause such child to receive efficient elementary instruction in reading, writing, and arithmetic, and if such parent fail to perform such duty, he shall be liable to such orders and penalties as are provided by the Act. (Section 4)

An employer could not employ a child under the age of ten, nor could he employ a child under the age of fourteen unless the child could produce a certificate of proficiency in the three subjects mentioned in Section 4 of the Act. There were statutory exceptions to the declared law, e.g. if the child lived more than two miles from the school there would be no compulsion to attend (Section 11), and Section 9 states that the local authority could exempt children from the age of eight from attending school 'for the necessary operation of husbandry and the ingathering of crops.'

In Commins Coch English was the language of the school despite the fact that all the children were monoglot Welsh. These were the days of the 'Welsh Not'. In 1975 I interviewed a farmer, John Ryder Griffiths, and he had a clear memory of his school days in Commins Coch. I asked him about the language of the school. 'English,' he said. 'The Headmaster told us that we came to school to learn English. "You have plenty of Welsh at home," he added.'

Some may say that the 'Welsh Not' had an educational value, but this has to be balanced against the effect on the survival of the language. One thing is certain – we had to be fluent in English if we were to succeed at secondary school level.

The school log book gives an insight into the history of the community. There are frequent references to infectious diseases, particularly measles and whooping cough. The school itself was one big room with a high ceiling, heated by two open fireplaces. Coal was in very short supply and the school was often without a fire. The school log book contains many items of historical interest which illustrate the interaction between the school and its environment, and the frequent references to the celebrations of local and national events relating to the British Empire:

29.6.1897 Received 25 [writing] slates into the school.

9.7.1897   The girls in Std III are well up in their work, but the boys are still backward.

9.7.1898   The farmers are busy now, and most of the children are kept at home to help.

5.1.1900   *Inspector's Report*: 'The upper standards . . . do not seem to understand the simplest questions in English. If I ask the meaning of any word they always give me the Welsh word for it and seem to think that it is all that is required. I have spoken to the Monitress regarding speaking English to the little ones, as she prefers giving her commands in Welsh.'

14.6.1900 School closed for today. Only 18 children present owing to celebration in the village of English entering Pretoria.

10.9.1900 A case of truancy was dealt with this afternoon. One lad (Edwin Davies) who absented himself this morning was punished – two strokes on the hand.

21.6.1902   *Inspector's Report*: 'The school has again suffered from change of teachers and from the prevalence of epidemic sickness in the neighbourhood. The new master seems to have done very good work since his advent. Praiseworthy discipline is maintained . . .'
School staff at time of above report: Headmaster, Sewing Mistress, Monitress, Monitor.

18.9.1902   School closed. A large fair held at Machynlleth. The children also go about to gather nuts on this day and consequently they call it 'Nutting Day'.

3.2.1903   The School Attendance Officer called this afternoon and made enquiries with regard to the attendance of Cemmaes Road children. The Registers were shown to him, and he could then see for himself how shockingly bad the attendance has been. He promised to see the parents . . . threaten them with legal proceedings unless matters will improve. It is quite true that they have close on two miles to walk along a bleak road . . .

1.3.1904   Children told a little about St. David and St. David's Day, and that Welshmen wear the leek on this day as an emblem of their nationality.

25.3.1904   Attendance should have been better, but I understand that several are unable to attend owing to eruption of the skin which has been prevalent now and again for the past two months. [This was probably impetigo.]

24.1.1905   Deem it advisable to send for a medical certificate authorising the closure of the school for the rest of the week. Feel so giddy that I could hardly stand on my feet. Whole families are laid up and all so sudden. The complaint is influenza.

22.6.1905   School closed – there are meetings at the Wesleyan chapel in connection with the revival.

7.2.1906   Received ½ ton of coal for school use . . . the coal is inferior in quality to the one usually received although the same price is charged.

2.3.1906   Received a letter from the Managers complaining that ½ ton of coal monthly is too much and require an explanation how it can possibly be used.

24.5.1906   Holiday. Empire Day.

30.4.1907   Number on books – 50.

26.6.1907   School closed in the afternoon owing to Machynlleth fair. These fairs play havoc with the attendance. The scholars do not go themselves, but are kept at home to do household duties, while their parents are away.

20.12.1907   School closed for the Christmas holiday. I have always noticed that the attendance for the week preceeding Christmas is very poor, as many of the scholars are kept at home to help with the feathering, etc.

20.5.1910   Funeral of King Edward VII. School closed in consequence by order of the Education Committee.

14.7.1910   School closed. The Wesleyans have their trip to Aberystwyth, and almost all my scholars belong to that denomination.

29.1.1912   The cold this morning was somewhat intense, the ink in the ink wells was actually frozen . . . an unprecedented occurrence since my advent, but I am glad to state that the fires in the school-room counteract its severity, and the scholars look happy and comfortable.

4.11.1912   Several absentees, as the steam thrasher is in a neighbouring farm and some of the children have gone there to assist in carrying water, etc.

7.2.1913   The weather was very unfavourable for the scholars, especially those who come from a distance, but invariably they attend better than those who live in the village.

10.11.1913   The lesson given by Mrs Lloyd in connection with tuberculosis was very interesting and instructive, and the scholars, as she remarked, were very attentive and seemed to appreciate what was told them.

[Note: All schools had been sent a circular letter on tuberculosis – and material for this lecture.]

28.9.1914 This morning the watch presented by the Education Committee to William John Davies – for 5 years unbroken attendance – reached me safely. (July 1st 1909 to June 30th 1914).

[The Watch was presented to William John Davies on 22.10.14. His record of attendance was a remarkable achievement. The records show that he was the Headmaster's son.]

10.5.1915 *H.M. Inspector's Report*: – A long report which includes the following items: 'This school is well managed, the children are clean, cheerful and orderly and are taught with creditable skill and industry ... much of the work done in arithmetic, handwriting and composition shows careful teaching . . . The use of Welsh as a medium of instruction especially in the lower divisions needs further development although more is now done than formerly. English and Welsh composition must be given alternatively, and on no account should the written translation exercises from English into Welsh and also from Welsh into English be omitted.'

[Note: a dent in the Welsh-Not rule.]

12.11.1917 It is with regret that I have to withdraw the name of one of my scholars – David Edward Humphreys – who has been drowned in the River Twymyn.

14.1.1918 This morning the lessons were chiefly devoted to the lives of our celebrated men – warriors, navigators and discoverers – who did so much in laying the foundation of our vast empire on which the sun never sets.

14.3.1919 Deemed it advisable to close for this afternoon, as several of the scholars after having trudged along through the slush and sleet are shivering all over from cold as there are no fires to warm them owing to a shortage of coal.

9.9.1919   Sir O.M. Edwards, senior school inspector of Wales, visited this morning when the scholars of the upper standards were reading about exploration of Africa by Dr Livingstone and Sir H.M. Stanley. Sir Owen stated that he knew the latter personality and gave a few very interesting facts concerning his early life which the children highly appreciated . . . He complimented me on my work, and remarked that he knew that I had to work very hard with only one supplementary.

11.11.1920 Two minutes silence for meditation in accordance with the Government's instructions to commemorate the signing of the Armistice. An address was afterwards delivered in connection with the same.

The Headmaster retired on 31 March 1921 after 19 years in the same post. There was a constant changing of teachers which added to the work of the Headmaster. Absenteeism continued to be a problem and, as usual, those who lived nearest to the school were the worse offenders. Farmers kept their children at home to help with the harvest, sheep shearing and potato picking.

A recurring complaint was lack of coal and there is a reference to children bringing firewood to the school so that they could have basic heat. On 19 October 1926 the temperature when the school opened was 39°F and an oil stove had to be borrowed to heat the room.

In 1924 it is apparent that tuberculosis was a problem in the area and specialist lecturers visited the school to address the children on 'Prevention of Tuberculosis'. There is frequent reference to outbreaks of measles and whooping cough, also 'spotted fever' which was probably chicken pox or maybe scarlet fever. In 1928 there was an epidemic of infective jaundice (hepatitis). In 1931, after much discussion, the schoolroom was divided in two by a partition. This had the added advantage of keeping the school warm because both sections had a fireplace.

The H.M.I. Report dated 3 July 1928 says:

> Taken as a whole this school impresses me favourably. In the composite upper group there is solid progress in the three R's . . . It is clear from the very sound standard attained in such aspects as singing, physical exercise, and nature study, that the scholars' interests are sufficiently varied . . . Practically all the children are Welsh speaking and the mother tongue receives attention in reading, recitations, singing and the terminal examinations. There appears however to be no reason why Welsh cannot be used as a medium of written expression generally as increasingly now is the practice in areas of this nature.

This appears to signify the end of the 'Welsh Not' – at least in this small rural school.

In March 1973 Commins Coch School, together with three other village schools, was closed and the children conveyed by bus to a new primary school in Glantwymyn (Cemmaes Road). The new school was officially opened by my uncle, Alderman Stanley Hughes, on 22 March 1973. I had the honour of being President at the social function on the same evening held in the new school hall.

From Commins Coch School I was accepted into Machynlleth County School, a secondary grammar school. Machynlleth was very 'English' in those days and we, the country folk, were still very 'Welsh'. The English-speaking children thought we were a bit *twp* (backward) but we caught up with them! I have already referred to the progressive Headmaster at the school, Mr Haddon Roberts, a strict disciplinarian and an excellent teacher of Chemistry. The motto of the school was appropriate: 'Lumen Nobis Sit Scienta' (Let Knowledge be Light). That became true for me and it still applies today.

CHAPTER 4

FROM MACHYNLLETH
TO ABERYSTWYTH 1939-1942

I left Machynlleth County School with reasonable School Certificate results at the end of the summer term in 1939. I clearly remember listening to the Prime Minister, Mr Neville Chamberlain, saying on the radio, 'this country is now at war with Germany.' I was then 17 and at the age of 18 men were likely to be called for military service. The question of what to do in life was an urgent problem. I had always wanted to be a vet, mainly because my father, in common with many other farmers, dealt with most of the ailments of the farm stock and I found it fascinating. My father made up medicines for things like *Dŵr Du* (Black urine) and *Dŵr Coch* (blood in the urine) in cattle and administered the drench by putting it in an old cow's horn, which he managed to get down the animals quite easily. He was also good at delivering calves and lambs that 'got stuck' at birth.

The only qualified vet I remember was a Mr Mills who lived in Caersws. The local farrier was known as Dan Farrier and he was a lay expert in attending to sick animals, especially horses. He travelled on a very old motorcycle and there were many times when he was too drunk to drive to his home in Llanbrynmair.

I remember my father operating on a sheep which had *bendro* (Staggers) – a deviation to the right or left when walking. He felt over the skull until he found a soft spot. Into this he pushed a trocar, a small silver-plated metal probe enclosed up to its point in a metal cannula. The trocar point would, with reasonable luck, pierce a collection of fluid in a Hydatid Cyst on the surface of the brain and this fluid would come out via the cannula when the trocar was removed. The small hole in the skull was then covered with 'Stockholm Tar' and the sheep would be well in a few days time. These cysts can appear in any part of the body in both humans and animals.

Dogs are often the hosts of the mature tapeworm and humans can be infected by eating unboiled vegetables soiled by dog excreta. If someone swallows the eggs they develop into embryos which penetrate the wall of the bowel and lodge in the organs of the body, such as the liver, lungs and spleen. There appears to be a reservoir of infection in the Montgomeryshire/Radnorshire border region and a more than average incidence of cysts in humans. This is a disease of sheep rearing areas, where men and dogs work closely together and the dogs are often infected by eating the flesh of dead infected sheep. I believe that it is most unwise to allow dogs to lick your face. You can guess where that tongue was a short time before!

In 1939 there was no question of my entering a veterinary college because there was only minimal recruitment at that stage of the war. In retrospect, I would not have qualified to enter a veterinary college because Physics was not taught in Machynlleth County School and I have no recollection of being taught Biology. Furthermore my parents could not afford to send me to college for five years, although they never said this to me, and I knew that I would, sooner or later, be called up for military service.

I was now looking for a job. By a stroke of good luck I saw an advertisement for a vacancy in Aberystwyth for an articled pupil in the Public Health Department. Mr Haddon Roberts, my Headmaster, strongly advised me to apply and I will always be indebted to him for this very sound and forward-looking professional advice. I applied and was accepted. An 'articled' pupil pays for his tuition. I paid £39 a year and my tutor and supervisor was the Public Health Inspector, Mr Osborne Evans, a dynamic personality with a very progressive outlook. And so, on 4 December 1939, I started my 'articles' in Aberystwyth – just one week before my 18th birthday.

I learnt a great deal in the Public Health Department about community health, something I have been involved in ever since. I had to learn about infectious diseases and isolation hospitals, fumigation of houses following a case of an infectious disease (in retrospect, a waste of time!), inspection of houses later described as unfit for human habitation, overcrowding, inspection of food premises, milk sampling (for added water and/or infection) and, much later, meat inspection. This meant an early morning visit to the local abattoir with my tutor until I became sufficiently competent to do the work myself. My diary for that time refers to frequent condemnation of meat because of tuberculosis.

Improvement of housing conditions was a priority in the Public Health Department. The Housing Act 1930 directed local authorities to clear or improve insanitary houses when classified as 'unfit for human habitation'. Mr Osborne Evans commenced a five-year slum clearance programme and I quote from his annual report for 1936 where he noted '4 or 5 children sleeping in one room.' Another case had 'children sleeping in the same room as parents, including a woman with advanced tuberculosis,' and 'A wife gave birth to a child in a bed which the district nurse stated was literally moving with bed bugs.'

Once a week it was my duty to visit the local Medical Officer of Health, Dr D.I. Evans, and give him the notifications of infectious diseases which had been received during the week. I saw him in his surgery, which is the room where I am now writing these words. The experience in the Public Health Department was a major help to me, not only in the Army Medical Service, but also in my approach to medical problems generally. I learnt to see the patient in his own environment and this approach was highlighted in the World Health Organisation definition of health: 'A state of physical, mental and social well-being and not merely the absence of disease or infirmity.'

One of my tasks was to take samples of milk, water, and ice-cream for bacteriological examination. This made me a very frequent visitor to the bacteriology department of the University in Aberystwyth where I met Mr S.B.Thomas who was head of the Department of Bacteriology. His laboratory handled all the bacteriological work for the Borough of Aberystwyth. After a time he persuaded me to enrol as a student in the University to study Dairy Bacteriology. He was able to arrange for me to blend the two jobs and this proved to be a most valuable experience for me. The lecturers in the department, S.B.Thomas and John Lewis, were not only excellent teachers but also perfect gentlemen. Dairy Bacteriology was part of the 'Dairying' course in the college and I spent time making cheese and butter, and I had to visit the college farm to learn how to milk! The training in Bacteriology was of immense value to me in later life and I continued to attend lectures until I was called up for military service in 1942.

As if I did not have enough to do, I got involved in helping out with the evacuees who were coming to Aberystwyth from Liverpool in the early months of the war. Osborne Evans was the Chief Billeting Officer and I did a lot of office work for him. It was his job to decide which houses had to accept the evacuees and how many. My diary entry for 11 February 1941 reads: '500 evacuees arrived in Aberystwyth today – 100 for the Borough. I helped with the billeting and finished about 10.00 pm.'

The evacuees brought a lot of illnesses with them, including scabies and impetigo. Tanybwlch Mansion had been taken over as an emergency isolation hospital and the Grand Hotel in Borth was later taken over as a skin infections hospital. The children settled down very well. They had their own teachers and Mr Evans had to co-ordinate all this work, which he did very well.

I also found time to join the college O.T.C. (Officers' Training Corps) which was good preparatory experience for the Army. I took my turn at fire watching at the top of the college tower in King Street. Enemy aircraft flew over this area *en route* to Liverpool and our main task was to ensure that no lights could be seen in the town. In my diary, the entry for 8 April 1941 reads: 'Air raid alert for 6 hours last night – until 4.00 am. Enemy aircraft over Aberystwyth.'

Prior to the introduction of the National Health Service in 1948 every local authority had its own Medical Officer of Health, who was usually a G.P. in the area. It was his statutory duty to oversee the health of the local population. He reported to the Council every month and produced an annual report. These reports are now in the National Library of Wales in Aberystwyth and make very interesting reading. The first report is dated 1897. In the early part of the 20th century infectious diseases claimed many lives, the main culprits being whooping cough, diphtheria, scarlet fever, meningitis, 'summer diarrhoea' and, above all, the 'Captain of the Men of Death', tuberculosis. The Infant Mortality Rate (I.M.R.) is a sensitive index of the health of the community as determined by social and economic influences. The index is calculated as follows:

$$\frac{\text{Number of infant deaths under 1 year of age}}{\text{Number of live births in the year}} \times 1000$$

In 1906 the I.M.R. for Aberystwyth Borough was 186. That means 32 children under one year old died in that year. The rate for England and Wales was 133. Today (year 2000) the rate for Wales is 6.1, Ceredigion is 4.5 and, for comparison, India 74 and Nigeria 72. The Medical Officer of Health, Dr Abraham Thomas, commented in his annual report for 1906 on the high I.M.R. in the Borough:

For a health resort like Aberystwyth with all its natural and hygienic advantages the infant mortality rate (I.M.R.) is considerably higher than even the large industrial centres of England.

Why should this be? There were three main factors – poverty, bad housing and tuberculosis. It was the function of a Public Health Department to attend to these matters. There is no doubt that the good health enjoyed by the people of Aberystwyth today is not due to doctors or antibiotics but to improvements in the environment – a good sewer, an efficient waste disposal system, clean dry houses with no overcrowding, clean water, safe milk, clean air, contraception leading to smaller families which means more money to buy proper food. I must also add immunisation against the killing diseases – whooping cough, measles, diphtheria and poliomyelitis. Some of these diseases have disappeared but could very easily appear again, as stated by Dr H.R. Tighe, one-time Medical Officer of Health for Swansea: 'Old diseases are ready to reappear when their long absence has made them unfamiliar and made man careless.'

As a result of local government re-organisation since 1948, the office of the local Medical Officer of Health has disappeared. This was a major mistake, equal to the loss of the Matron in our hospitals!

One story to close the chapter. Taking samples of milk served two purposes: bacteriological examination and testing for added water. A Cardiganshire man selling milk in London said to one of his customers, 'I have a new cow and this one produces nine quarts of milk every day.'

'How much of that do you sell?' asked the customer.

'Twelve quarts,' was the quick reply.

CHAPTER 5

ARMY SERVICE 1942-47

In my last year in Aberystwyth I daily expected a call from the King – that brown envelope with the words 'On His Majesty's Service' printed at the top. I had my medical examination in 1941 and passed A1. Mr Osborne Evans asked for the postponement of my call-up because of the work I was doing with the evacuees. I was granted six months extension. Early in July the call for duty duly arrived and on 16 July 1942 I left Commins Coch, never really to return there for any length of time. My father took me in the car to Cemmaes Road Station to catch the train. As the train passed through Commins Coch I waved to my mother and to the dozens of villagers who had assembled to wave me off. I did not see my father again because he died about six months later from cancer of the stomach, at the age of 54. I had compassionate leave to attend his funeral. I was 20 years old.

The train arrived in Fleet, Hampshire, in the late evening and masses of young men carrying cases emerged on to the platform. We were a new 'intake' and were loaded into army lorries and taken to Boyce Barracks near Aldershot. Next day we were issued with army uniform, that included an itchy shirt. We were not allowed to wear a vest and our civilian clothes were sent home. During my two months or so in Boyce Barracks we had basic military training and educational tests followed by interviews, which would determine to which branch of the army each of us would be posted. Fortunately my past training and experience led to my being posted to the Royal Army Medical Corps (R.A.M.C.).

My time in Boyce Barracks came to an end and I was very

pleased to be sent to the Army School of Hygiene (A.S. of H.). This again was in the Aldershot area and more like a college than barracks. I joined a two-month course on Military Hygiene – not far removed from what I was doing in Aberystwyth. One of the officers, Major H.H. Clay, was the author of a textbook which I had used in Aberystwyth! It was a most interesting course and I am glad to say that I passed the examinations. More luck came my way: I was promoted to the rank of Corporal and made an Instructor at the A.S. of H, one of about 30 N.C.O.s on the staff. The school ran courses for soldiers from all branches of the service; they came for a 12-day course every 14 days. The lectures we gave were accompanied by practical demonstrations on such things as refuse disposal, prevention of fly infestation (very important), water purification, mosquito control, prevention of skin infections, construction of septic tanks, etc.

The Army Manual defined Hygiene as the science of the maintenance and promotion of health and the prevention of disease. Sanitation was defined as the practical application of the science of hygiene to the varied conditions of life. Clean water is always a problem in the Army, especially overseas when, too often, the only water available is from wells which have dead animals and other refuse at the bottom. The Army had four-wheeled 15 cwt water trucks. These had two filters through which the pumped water had to travel and the water was then chlorinated and tested frequently for its purity. The water tank carried 230 gallons of water. The filters would withhold 90% of impurities including the ova of Entamoeba Histolytica (which gave rise to serious anaemia and gastro-enteritis in tropical areas). Every member of the class had to be examined. If they passed, which the majority did, they would be the Hygiene men in their particular units.

I was at the A.S of H. until the Second Front in June 1944, when the bulk of the teaching ceased and we, the instructors, were available for posting to active service units. I narrowly missed a posting to the 6th Airborne Division. Two of us were interviewed, both A1, aged 21 and single. Fortunately I was not chosen. Cpl

Harries had to go and he was killed when the glider he was in landed on a minefield in France.

During my stay at the A.S. of H. my thoughts were yet again on entering a Veterinary college and I went to see the Army Education Officer. He advised me to take a correspondence course in Biology whilst in the army, study Physics after the war, and then apply. The correspondence course followed me to the end of my time in the army.

One day a notice appeared on the 'Orders' board – all corporal instructors to report to Company Office at mid-day. We were told, 'You are all posted overseas and you leave today on seven days embarkation leave. You report to Boyce Barracks at the end of your leave and move to operational units from there.'

We expected something like this but not quite so suddenly! I packed my kit, said 'goodbye' to many, and travelled by train to London, then to Crewe, and home on the early Mail train. My mother did not expect me because we were sworn to secrecy about our movements. My embarkation leave passed quickly and the time came for me to say 'goodbye' again. I had no idea where I would land up, but my first port of call was Boyce Barracks as instructed. After waiting for about five days, hundreds of us, from all Army units, were told to dress in 'full-kit' and assemble at 2.00 pm on the barrack square. A Sergeant Major got up on a box and told us, in typically loud fashion, that we would be travelling that night by train to 'somewhere'.

'Three things I have to say to you,' he said. 'Make sure that you have made your will.' We all had blank copies for this. 'Check that the disc around your neck has your Army number on it and your religion. If you have no religion you will be buried C. of E.' Thirdly he said, 'You obey orders. It is not for you to question why. It is for you to do or die.'

Many years afterwards when I was doing research for my PhD I investigated the question of consent when in the Forces. It became a subject for discussion because the British soldiers who fought in the Gulf War (1990-91) were subjected to a battery of injections, some of which had not been tested beforehand owing to the urgency of the situation. They could not refuse. After the war some of the troops have suffered from 'Gulf War Syndrome' which has included their children being born with congenital malformations. Informed consent is not yet a feature of army life.

From Boyce Barracks, we were taken in Army transport to Fleet station and got on to a long troop train which was all blacked out. Armed soldiers were on the platform. We travelled all night, six to a carriage, very comfortably, and when dawn came we found ourselves racing through Scotland. We passed through Glasgow and arrived in Gourock, where a tender took us to a troop ship, the *Highland Chieftain*. We went on board and were taken to a troop deck well below the water line. This was a banana boat in peacetime and the troop decks were full of refrigeration pipes from which we hung our hammocks. We had to sleep in our clothes and life jacket. We were in Gourock for five days and on the sixth day woke to realise that the ship was moving. From the deck I saw that we were in a convoy of twenty ships with a strong escort. It was on board that I met one of my fellow instructors from the A.S. of H., Albert Lloyd, and discovered that he and I were on the same destination draft – E.1. We were issued with Mepacrine anti-malarial tablets. On the fifth day I woke up and was aware that the ship had stopped and when I went on deck I saw the lit-up Rock of Gibraltar. It was still dark but after dawn I saw Gibraltar in all its glory.

We left Gibraltar the next day in a convoy of three big ships with an escort. Nine corporals, including Lloyd and I, were detailed for police duty on board. We slept in cabins (a luxury!) and lived in the Guard Room. The order came to change to trop-ical dress and we now guessed that we were going to West Africa – hence the anti-malaria tablets. Seven days later we sailed into Freetown harbour and saw West Africa for the first time. Many 'bum boats' came alongside. We threw money into the sea and the Africans would dive after it. The heat was severe. This was November, the start of the dry season. We sailed to destination

E.1., Takoradi in Ghana (called Gold Coast at that time). We disembarked and were taken to a Transit Camp, very comfortable but very hot. Next day all the troops were taken to Takoradi station and travelled by train to Kumasi, arriving at 3.00 am. Lloyd and I had to split here – he went on to Accra and I sat on the platform on my own, waiting for someone to collect me.

Before long an African soldier took me to the 'Imperial Mess' where I had breakfast, and later was collected by an Army Medical Officer who took me to my destination – the 52nd West African General Hospital. My duties were to inspect and monitor the sanitary state of the hospital, with special emphasis on anti-malarial precautions. I had an African assistant and a civilian foreman who supervised 162 men working in the hospital, maintaining a high standard of hygiene. I was the first to be appointed to this post and the work I was doing was not unlike my work in the Public Health Department in Aberystwyth. Kumasi was a reasonable colonial town with a good British infrastructure. It had a very nice YMCA for the troops, staffed by Europeans, mainly wives of UK workers in the area. I was a frequent visitor to the YMCA and I met many A.S. of H. men there, members of the 43rd Field Hygiene Section based on Kumasi. The YMCA had a reading room and I made good use of that. My diary for 11 December 1944 states: 'I sat in the reading room most of the evening. I picked up one of the periodicals and read an article headed: "Why Aberystwyth means so much to Wales."'

The accommodation I had was very pleasant with plentiful fruit growing in the hospital garden, grapefruit, bananas and pineapples. I settled down to work and enjoyed it. Dysentery was much too prevalent in the hospital. I arranged for all the hospital cooks to be examined and three were found to be carriers of the germ.

Soon after arriving in Kumasi I was asked, with others, to take part in a trial of a new anti-malarial drug called Paludrine. I had to take Mepacrine as well for two weeks then Paludrine alone. It was no good – I was in hospital with malaria within a month. That was the first of three or four attacks I had in West Africa. Having malaria myself made me redouble the anti-malarial measures around the hospital. Fly infestation was also a problem and my workmen built a very efficient incinerator which helped a lot. Paludrine was withdrawn but after modification it became a most useful and efficient anti-malarial drug in the years after the war.

We had to dress in long trousers, shirt with a tie, long boots with trousers tucked into them. We also had to cover our hands and face with an anti-mosquito cream which had a horrible smell. This mode of dressing had to start just before the sun went down. We always slept under a mosquito net and this had to be in situ before dusk when the mosquitoes became active in the search for food – our blood! I had good news at this time when I was promoted to the rank of Sergeant. I also continued with my biology course.

It was soon obvious to me that we were not winning the war against mosquitoes. Malaria among European soldiers was increasing. I found mosquitoes breeding in the 'bush' about half a mile from the hospital. The hospital entomologist and I found very many small pools in a swampy area, and the water was full of mosquito larvae. Our labour force duly drained the swamp. Kumasi is a relatively wet area with thick forest regions and mosquitoes are able to breed with impunity.

I heard a rumour that I was going to be transferred to the 43rd Field Hygiene Section. I was sorry to hear this because I liked working in the hospital and the Colonel-in-charge did not want me to go, but orders are to be obeyed. On 27 January 1945 I was duly transferred.

Next day something happened which changed my life completely (looking at it in retrospect). The Field Hygiene Section was ordered to dispatch immediately a batch of senior NCOs to the Northern Territories to help control a serious epidemic of cerebro-spinal meningitis which could easily spread south and involve troops of the Royal West African Frontier Force training for action in the Far East. There was a mad rush to get all our equipment together. We had four army lorries plus a water purification truck and a plentiful supply of water purification tablets. We left Kumasi on 28 January 1945; my diary entry reads:

> We travelled along narrow dusty roads bounded by high trees and thick undergrowth. I have to act as Quartermaster on the trip and my most urgent job will be to look after the rations.

Corned beef and army biscuits were our standard meal. We had to camp overnight, sleeping in the lorries. Off we went in the morning. It was very hot, dusty and dry as we got nearer to the desert. This was an area of scrubland which merged with the Sahara at its northern end. After a journey of about 300 miles we arrived in a town called Wa – home to a resident colonial doctor, Dr Brown, and the District Commissioner. A Veterinary Surgeon (European) lived close by and he and I had a lot to talk about! Wa was the only town of any size in the Northern Territories. It had a large market and many roads leading to it. It had a small hospital and a school and, at that time, was said to have about 8,000 inhabitants. There was a Syrian trader with a shop in the town and he was a great help to the Army. We sorted out accommodation for the African soldiers and we Europeans took over the 'rest house'. One of our army drivers acted as our cook and I don't think he had ever cooked anything before! Ultimately our Steward Boys took over the cooking. We had one hurricane lamp for a light and massive flying ants would surround this at night. Dr Brown invited us British NCOs to his house for a meal and then explained what we had to do. My diary entry reads:

> 28.1.45. The plan of campaign was explained to us. Numerous cases of meningitis are being reported and treated by Dr Brown. The total number of reported cases is 400 with about 28 deaths.

We studied a map of the district and we decided to place our men in the isolated villages and teach them to recognise cases of meningitis (quite easy because meningitis then was 'true to form') and treat the victims with sulphanilamide tablets, basically M and B

693, according to a schedule which allowed for the age and size of the patient. In the case of children the tablets were dissolved in boiled, cooled water. They took this quite readily, probably because they were very thirsty. Dr Brown performed lumbar punctures early on but there was no time or need to do this in every case. The men we posted into the villages were highly intelligent African NCOs. They had the title 'Dispensers' and were equivalent in knowledge and expertise to the Ward Sisters in the UK – and you can't have a higher standard than that.

My job, with others, was to visit them every other day, collect reports on the cases and top up the supply of tablets. The weather was very hot and dry, this being the 'dry' season. It got quite cold at night with the temperature of about 103°F at mid-day dropping to about 70°F at night. This was a problem because the villagers huddled together in their 'mud compound' houses which were grossly overcrowded and had no light or ventilation, apart from a doorway through which one had to crawl to enter the rooms. The disease spread rapidly under these conditions because it is passed by droplet infection.

Once we were properly organised, my European colleagues returned to Kumasi and I was left on my own, working all the time in consultation with Dr Brown. I had quite a big unit of African soldiers, and I had to look after them and also the vehicles. Getting petrol from Kumasi proved a problem and the money to pay the soldiers was never on time. I ate well because I was given guinea fowls and eggs in every village I visited. My transport consisted of a Jeep and a motor cycle. I mainly used the Jeep, with an African driver, because the 'roads' were so bad that riding a motor cycle was dangerous, although I did use it sometimes to save petrol. The Jeep was open-topped and had no side doors but it was sturdy and dependable.

It soon became obvious that we were getting nowhere in controlling the epidemic because we could not isolate the victims. The mud huts had a flat roof (see the picture in the plate section) and I suggested that the occupants should sleep on the roof, but that did not work because it was too cold at night. It was at this stage that I had an idea. My diary entry explains:

> 8.2.45. – Visited a village . . . interviewed the Chief. I explained through an interpreter that we wanted to cure the 'sickness'. I asked for his co-operation and said that a grass hospital should be built outside the village. The Chief agreed and his men started straight away.

A 'grass hospital' has cubicles separated by screens of tall elephant-type grass: one patient to each cubicle, lying on a grass mat and looked after by one relative. The 'Dispenser' would be in charge. This set-up was repeated in many villages and proved a great success.

Getting clean water was always a problem and I was often very thirsty. The Syrian trader suggested buying some 'Peto' wine which the natives made. This was sterile, having been boiled for some time, and I filled my water bottle with this whenever I could. The water in the few still operative wells was so filthy that I had to super-chlorinate the water after pumping it through the filters. Tea tasted horrible! Dr Brown also came to our rescue in that he had a supply of canned beer. We drank this half water and half beer. He also allowed us to use his well water which was not contaminated.

I travelled many miles every day in the Jeep visiting the village 'hospitals' and recording the number of cases and deaths. I had to put a handkerchief over my nose and mouth when travelling in the Jeep or on my motor cycle because of the fine red dust in the atmosphere. The handkerchief would be red after an hour or so. I was convinced that this dry dust, plus thirst, was a major factor in spreading the disease because the germ lodges in the throat. I expanded on this idea in my final report on the epidemic.

As I have said before, I had an African soldier driver for the Jeep. One day we went on to a wooden bridge, which collapsed, sending the Jeep into the dried-up riverbed. Fortunately it landed on its wheels. A group of strong men from a nearby village got the

Jeep out of the riverbed with very little effort. The only damage was a bent front leaf spring. The Jeep had to be sent back to base and I had a brand new Jeep in exchange. Although I had my motor cycle, it was of limited use because I could not take an interpreter on it with me.

By February 1945 the number of cases had reached 1,300 with 180 deaths. I was visiting bush hospitals every day and that sometimes involved a journey of 70-80 miles. It became necessary for me to use my motor cycle more and more because we were always short of petrol and I had to borrow some from the Syrian trader. He was a most helpful man. A new doctor, Dr Waddy, arrived on the scene to relieve Dr Brown. I got on very well with Dr Waddy. He appreciated the help the Army was able to provide and we, in turn, were interested in the work and were very happy to do it. The number of cases of meningitis continued to rise but we were able to stop its spread to the military training area of Ashanti (Kumasi being the Capital). I recorded in my diary: '18.2.1945: 161 new cases reported today. Total cases now 2146 with 296 deaths.'

I started compiling a graph of the cases as they appeared daily, relating this to the relative humidity as recorded every day. The relative humidity was very low – as low as 26% most days. It was only when this rose, with the approach of the wet season, that the number of new cases dropped. The low relative humidity increased the dryness of the throat in all of us.

The work went on in spite of the difficulty of obtaining enough petrol, long delays in getting money to pay the soldiers, and increasing difficulty of getting clean water. We had plenty of food – too many chickens and guinea fowl! – all given by the village chiefs as gifts. The epidemic continued and I kept my graphs up to date. My diary entry for 1 April 1945 reads: 'Number of cases now 8000, but treated deathrate 8.07%. A little rain today. Much colder now.'

I became ill with a recurrence of malaria but got better in three days after increasing the Mepacrine. The water situation became very serious. It would take an hour to get a reasonable quantity of water. Relief came when it started to rain following a violent thunderstorm, and the local people could be heard giving thanks to Allah. Many high-ranking doctors came to Wa to discuss the epidemic and the DDMS (Deputy Director of Medical Services) liked my graphs and was very impressed by the grass hospitals put up in one day outside a village. The wet season arrived and the epidemic of meningitis came to an end. Total cases recorded by me: 9,385. Deaths 1,026. Untreated deaths 279. Total Mortality 11.05%. Treated Mortality 8.05%.

The war in Europe came to an end on 6 May 1945. I received instructions to withdraw all army medical personnel and return to Kumasi. We had no wireless but the day before we heard on the 'Bush Telegraph' that the German forces in Europe had surrendered. I brought in all our men from the bush 'hospitals' and packed our lorries ready to depart. The rain had filled the wells and it was easy to get water at last. I got permission from GHQ to stay an extra day in Wa so that we could celebrate victory in the bush. My diary entry for 8 May 1945 is as follows:

V.E. Day: At 11.30 am I headed 12 men from the Hygiene Section and marched to the Union Jack Grandstand. The paramount Chief and all his subordinate chiefs, all in brightly coloured clothes, gathered around. The Police and school children were also there. The District Commissioner (DC) and Brigadier Findlay inspected the men. A short speech by the DC who announced the end of the war in Europe. The school children then sang 'God Save the King'. I marched my men past the Flagpole and saluted the Flag. After the ceremony we were all invited to the DC's house and had lunch with him. It was pointed out to the hundreds of Africans assembled here today that their men cannot come home until the Japanese war is over. At 7.30 tonight the King spoke and we all gathered around the (repaired) wireless under a hurricane lamp. Reception was perfect . . . Natives dancing outside. Drums beating. So ends a dramatic V.E. Day.

Next day we left Wa, and after a hundred mile trip stayed in a town called Kintampo. What luxury to have clean water coming out of a tap! We should never object to paying the water rate in the UK. How nice it would have been to have a bottle of Tŷ Nant water in the desert! Next day the convoy arrived in Kumasi. My diary entry for 10 April 1945 reads:

Started off on the long road to Kumasi . . . very dangerous road but the driver knows the road. The soldiers were singing as we entered Kumasi. Flags decorated all the streets and everybody had the victory spirit. All the Field Hygiene Sergeants came out to welcome us back. Had a wonderful dinner in the Imperial Mess.

Next day there was a thanksgiving service in the hospital which was attended by all the hospital staff. My final report on the Wa epidemic was dated 22 April 1945. At the end of the report I wrote:

How the epidemic spread is not known, but the following factors must be considered:

1   Low rainfall.
2   Very low relative humidity during the epidemic period compared with the average for the past 5 years.
3   Unsatisfactory housing conditions (overcrowding).
4   Low resistance to infection due to shortage of food in the dry season.
5   The atmosphere filled with fine dust particles constantly irritating the naso-pharynx.
6   Kola traders being suspected carriers. (Carrier rate not known.)

My report concluded:

It is possible that a more serious epidemic will break out during the next dry Harmattan season, and it is hoped that the experience gained in this epidemic will help to cut down the number of cases and deaths next year.

The Department of Information in Accra produced a news-sheet called *The Empire at War* and I quote from the June 1945 edition which referred to the Wa epidemic:

> The present epidemic has in its severity and its extent completely eclipsed all former records ... It has taken a heavy toll of life, and but for the relief which modern medicines have afforded and the speed with which the civil Government and the Army brought them to the people, there can be no doubt that the area would have been completely devastated.

My report on the meningitis epidemic in Wa plus maps and graphs were brought up to date and given to my commanding officer, Major Bamber, for onward transmission to General Headquarters in Accra. I kept a carbon copy of my report and 55 years later, on 28 June 2000, I deposited all the documents I had relative to the epidemic in the Army Medical Services Museum in Keogh Barracks (the present day RAMC Depot).

I said earlier that in Africa 'something happened which changed my life completely.' Simply stated, I gave up the idea of being a vet and decided to be a doctor. This was going to be my aim from that time onwards.

I was back in Kumasi and my main task (yet again!) was to try and control the mosquito breeding because malaria was rampant and the Army could not afford to have so many British soldiers in hospital when they were needed in the Far East. Flies were also a problem and dysentery was a common ailment spread by flies. I also taught a new intake of African soldiers the basic elements of military hygiene. I became ill again with malaria and was admitted to hospital but got over it in less than a week.

The Army decided to reduce military training in West Africa and the Field Hygiene Section, of which I was a member, was disbanded. I was posted to Accra and attached to the 37(WA) General Hospital. This was a big hospital with nice accommodation. I was issued with a motor cycle and told to report to the Inter-Allied Malaria Control Group. 'Inter-Allied' means a joint effort from the British, American, Canadian, and Colonial

Services. I spent a lot of time in the Entymological Laboratory and my task was to classify mosquitoes caught at various places during the previous night, and mark on a big wall map where the anopheles mosquitoes were breeding. The Royal Engineers dealt with the breeding areas. The lagoons around Accra caused trouble and these were sprayed with 'Paris Green' which blocked the breathing tubes of the larvae.

Life is never static in the Army. I was ordered by GHQ back to Kumasi to join a small party, under Major Bamber, who were returning to Wa to research into the meningitis epidemic. We were now in the wet season (July 1945) and my diary entry said:

> Wa looks very different in the wet season. Heavy rain every day – plenty of water everywhere and even green grass grows.

Our task was to swab the throats of a sample of children in the area and also to investigate the average diet of the children and how this differed in the dry/wet seasons. We took swabs from about 120 children a day and these were cultured in our mobile bacteriological laboratory. The roads were a sea of mud and mosquitoes were everywhere. We also tested the children for Bilharzia and found 23% of the sample testing positive. We visited the White Fathers Mission (a Canadian Catholic Mission) and obtained a lot of information about the food consumed, when available. We were told about, and shown, leaves and wild fruit used in native soups. We took samples for chemical examination later.

Readers will have guessed by now that I kept a diary when overseas. Two further entries may be of interest:

> 20.7.45: I put my hat, [Bush hat essential for sun protection,] on the roof of my car when in a village and left it on the roof. I only discovered this when I returned to Wa. [My hat was found by the police and returned to me.]

> 22.7.45: One of the Steward Boys dropped some curry powder on the sugar and spoilt it. [Sugar, a precious

commodity, was in very short supply and we had to do without it until we returned to Kumasi.]

Wa was a most unhealthy place in the wet season and I can quite understand why the Gold Coast (Ghana) was referred to as the 'White Man's Grave'. When our mission was complete we returned to Kumasi. When we arrived there we heard that the Labour Party had won the election with a large majority. Mr Churchill had resigned and Mr Attlee was the new Prime Minister. I expected to be sent back to Accra but GHQ wanted me to stay in Kumasi and help control the mosquito breeding (once again!). In addition to my normal duties I was made Paymaster for the Kumasi area. This was quite a responsibility because I was handling a lot of money, about £600. I had to deal with a lot of queries about the pay of the African soldiers. Some were making voluntary deductions from their pay in favour of a wife but would want to change their wife! They could not write and had to enlist the services of a 'letter writer' who had no clue at all.

Despite all my problems good news came on 10 August 1945.

Greatest news of the war. Japan has asked for surrender terms. The news came through when we were in the YMCA. 'Music while you work' was on the wireless. It suddenly stopped and the announcer said – 'This is London calling Africa' and went on to give the good news. Everybody went wild. The news soon spread to the Africans and they were overjoyed.

15.8.45: This is V-J day. The great news came through on the first news broadcast this morning. The Emperor of Japan broadcast the surrender terms. Mr Attlee (Prime Minister) gave the news to the people of Britain . . . free tea and cakes in the YMCA. Special V-J party in the hospital tonight during which Taffy Rees sang 'Hen Wlad Fy Nhadau'.

This news was of particular importance to all of us serving in West Africa because this was the prime training ground for the Far East war. The Army led a march-past in Kumasi and the Chief

Commissioner for Ashanti took the salute. Also in the parade were schoolchildren, nurses, town council, Girl Guides and many others. On the following Sunday there was a thanksgiving service attended by all available soldiers and Europeans living locally. The Church was overflowing, with the Africans prominent in their colourful clothes.

The war was over but our work in the Army continued. The Hygiene Section was disbanded on 30 August 1945. I was posted to the Command Hygiene Section in Nigeria but was permanently attached to 37(WA) General Hospital in Accra. I liked this very much. My diary entry dated 6 September 1945 states: 'It is nice to be back in Accra again – this fresh sea breeze is just perfect.'

In Accra I had to concentrate on anti-malarial duties, inspecting army cookhouses with bacteriological testing of the people who worked there, testing the water supply, and also inspecting the hotels used by troops (including the YMCA). This is because there was a lot of bacillary dysentery on the campus. I was also given the job of meat inspection at the pig farm which supplied the troops.

I now had to consider my future once again. I wrote to the Medical College in Cardiff for details of entry and opportunities for ex-service men. On 12 October 1945 my diary entry reads:

Received long awaited letter from the Welsh School of Medicine in Cardiff. My school certificate will be accepted provided I reach matriculation standard in Biology. An application form was enclosed.

The Army Education Officer interviewed me and he arranged for me to attend classes in Biology at a local African college, Achimota College. The Principal of the college interviewed me and he was most helpful. His wife, Mrs Joselin, taught Biology. I attended my first lecture in Biology on 17 November 1945 at 07.30 hrs, followed by a practical class at 08.30 hrs. With the full support of my senior officers I went to college on my motor cycle. Mrs Joselin was a gifted teacher and very kind to me. I was invited many times to dinner in the evening followed by a session of classical music which I pretended to enjoy!

It was at one of these events that I met Miranda Huxtable, who came from South Wales. Mrs Huxtable sang very often on the local radio and Mr Huxtable was the Engineer-in-Charge of the Radio Station. They were very kind to me and often invited me to their house for dinner. At the time of my writing this, January 2001, both are alive and living in Chepstow.

I was very busy at work. Gastroenteritis was a major problem. Flies were everywhere and I got the Engineers to make covers for the latrines used by the natives in the bush just outside Accra. Very many cases of dysentery occurred in patients when they were in hospital, which suggested a source of infection there. The hospital pathologist joined me one day in a very thorough inspection of the hospital. We visited the food stores and food preparation areas and found rat droppings galore and one live mouse in the cookhouse. We found the source of the infection: it was one of the cooks who had missed or avoided testing. A bar attendant also tested positive. The mouse was innocent!

Anti-malarial work continued and the meat inspection at the pig farm had to be done in the evening before the meat went out the next day. At one stage the Army was concerned about a disease called Trichinosis. The disease is caused by a nematode (round worm) and the encysted larval form of the parasite is seen in the muscles of the pig. The affected muscles appear to be covered with fine white particles like sawdust and this is easily seen in the diaphragm. I took samples of the diaphragm in all the pigs I inspected and examined them in the hospital laboratory. They were all negative. I condemned a few carcasses of pigs because of tuberculosis.

I had good news on 4 December 1945. The diary notes: 'The Officer Commanding informed me today that I had been promoted Staff/Sergeant and backdated to September which will mean considerable back-pay.' But soon afterwards I had even better news.

19.1.46: Received the best news of the war – the award of the British Empire Medal – BEM (Mil.) for my work in Wa during the epidemic of meningitis. It appears that my name appeared in the New Year Honours List 1946.

In May 1946 I received a letter from the Medical School stating that I would have to attend for an interview in Cardiff but no date was given. I saw the Commanding Officer and together we drafted a letter to GHQ requesting compassionate return to the UK, the reason simply to allow me to attend for interview at the Medical College. GHQ approved immediately (which was unusual). I passed the three examinations I sat at Achimoto College and was given a certificate stating that I had achieved Matriculation standard in Biology. The time had now come for me to return home. On 23 May 1946 I recorded in my diary:

Notification came through today that a relief for me will arrive from Kaduna in the near future.

I had long known that the term 'in the near future' means nothing in the Army. However GHQ told me that the next boat for RHE (Reversion to Home Establishment) would leave on 1 July. My relief arrived on 7 June 1946 and my task then was to show him the range of duties expected of him, and he accompanied me on all my visits and inspections.

My embarkation documents came and I was due to sail on 1 July 1946 – actually I did not embark until 7 July. There was now the pleasant yet painful matter of saying goodbye to my friends, both military and civilian. We left Accra station and the band sounded the Last Post! The train arrived in Kumasi, we had a meal in the Sergeant's Mess, picked up more men, then off to Takoradi camp (the camp in which I spent my first night on the Gold Coast).

We were in the Transit Camp for five days and on 7 July 1946 embarked on the *Cheshire* (11,000 tons) sleeping in hammocks on the Mess decks. The ship was grossly overcrowded and had on board a lot of men returning from Burma. As the ship left the port, the band on the Quay played 'Auld Lang Syne' and 'Will ye no come back again?' and the time had come for me to say goodbye to the Gold Coast.

Looking back on my war service I was lucky to have spent my time in West Africa. I worked hard and carried a heavy responsibility, but the experience gained at an early age proved invaluable to me in the years ahead. The voyage home was uneventful and we soon had to change from tropical kit to battle dress because of the cold. We were due to land in Liverpool but actually docked in Glasgow and disembarked on 22 July. I arrived home on the early morning mail train on 25 July. As my last diary entry said: 'My diary of foreign service now comes to an end.'

At the end of my leave I was ordered to report to the Royal Herbert Hospital, Woolwich, London. This was a very old military hospital and my job there was a 'Wardmaster' in the Surgical Division. This meant organising the office, appointments, arranging medical boards for war casualties and preparing the operating lists as directed by the head of the Surgical Division, Lt. Col. S.M. Vassallo, a brilliant surgeon and a real gentleman.

I was called to Cardiff for an interview and to my great delight I was accepted as a medical student to start on 1 October 1946. An immediate problem arose, which worried me a great deal. I was not due for discharge until December and the Army refused to release me to go to college in October. The Medical College could not guarantee a place the following year. I would have to have another interview. I then decided to make good use of this time and volunteered to stay in the Army for another six months, until June 1947. During this time I attended evening classes at Woolwich Polytechnic studying Physics and Chemistry. I felt that I had forgotten my Chemistry, and Physics was new to me. It was an excellent college with very keen, older than average students. I applied again for admission to the Medical College, was interviewed and accepted. What a relief. I left the Army in May 1947.

> 'Rôl blino treiglo pob tref,
> Teg edrych tuag adref.

Mrs Win Davies of Aberystwyth was kind enough to translate the above for me:

> Now tired of the need to roam,
> How sweet becomes the thought of home.

CHAPTER 6

MEDICAL SCHOOL

When I was accepted as a medical student I was still in the Army. I had one final hurdle. Would I be able to have a grant from the Army to go to college? It was generally accepted that if a service man had had his studies interrupted by military service he would qualify for a grant. I applied and was asked to attend for interview at the offices of the Ministry of Labour in Cardiff. I duly attended, in my uniform. The interviewer was a lady. She could see from my notes that I had just come from the Gold Coast (Ghana) and she said that her husband had been a District Commissioner in Nigeria. When home on leave he had an operation to correct a deformity, the result of an injury in the First World War. He died on the table at the age of 36. She asked me about life on the Gold Coast and seemed very interested in all I had to say. She looked at my papers and said, 'That is all. Good luck. You will hear from us soon.'

I discovered some years later that my interviewer was Mrs Dora Herbert Jones, a distinguished civil servant. She was persuaded to join the staff at the famous Gregynog Press in Montgomeryshire, owned by the two Davies sisters of Gregynog. When one of the sisters died of leukaemia, the Press closed down, but has since re-established itself. Mrs Dora Herbert Jones then rejoined the Civil Service and in 1944 became head of the 'Further Education and Training Scheme' covering the whole of Wales.

The letter from the Ministry of Labour came a few days after my interview in Cardiff. Good news! I had been awarded a grant and this was a great relief.

The army grant was calculated to be adequate and was subject to the student passing the examinations. If we failed at the end of the first year the grant would stop permanently. We lost some excellent men at the end of the first year because they failed the examination. I felt very sorry for them because they had spent five years in the Forces and in that first year we had to take Physics, Chemistry, Botany and Zoology. One of my friends in the first year, Douglas Henderson, failed in Physics and had to leave college. He had been a Major in the Indian Army and fought in Burma. I was afraid of Physics but passed.

I liked the other subjects, especially Zoology. By happy coincidence one of the questions in the Zoology examination was 'Describe the life cycle of the malarial parasite and its relationship to the mosquito'! My correspondence course in Biology and my study in Achimota College proved invaluable. In the second and third year we studied Anatomy and Physiology, with the addition of Organic Chemistry in the second year and Physical Anthropology in the third year. I graduated BSc at the end of the third year and entered into the study of clinical medicine for the next three years. Here we were introduced to the day-to-day work of the doctor and during these years the ex-service men did very well. We worked very hard and spent a lot of our 'free' time helping out in Casualty and in the Post-Mortem (PM) room. The Nurses Home was 'out of bounds' to us!

Post-Mortem examination started at mid-day, every day, and I spent a lot of time there. After a while the doctor in charge, who was also the Home Office Pathologist, asked me whether I would like to have 'hands on experience' and I then took part in the post-mortem examinations under his supervision. This training was put to good use in later years when the then Pathologist in Aberystwyth did not like post-mortems, and I did all the post-mortems in Mid-Wales for about twelve years until a new Pathologist was appointed. The average number of PMs I did was about 60 a year, but one year I did 98. This meant that I was a frequent visitor to the Coroner's court because the vast majority of

PMs were sudden deaths – heart attacks, fatal strokes, accidents in the home and on the roads, suicide, falling off the cliff, sudden infant death, etc.

In addition to medical studies many of us attended medical conferences in other medical schools through active participation in the British Medical Students Association. I was Chairman of the Midland Region of the Association (Birmingham, Bristol, Oxford and Cardiff). Gwyn Thomas of Denbigh followed me as Chairman. He was, and still is, a great character!

The six years came to an end and I qualified as a doctor in 1953. My first post-graduate appointment was as House Physician in Paediatrics under Professor Watkins. I worked for six months in the Royal Infirmary in Cardiff and six months in Llandough Hospital. I clearly remember the paediatric wards in Llandough being full of children with rheumatic fever, a disease which has now almost disappeared. My pay for the first six months was £50 and £100 for the second six months, plus food. In my second post-graduate year I was appointed House Surgeon to Mr Hugh Jones, an exceptionally able surgeon and a nice man. This was in Llandough Hospital, where I was also House Surgeon to Mr Robert Owen, head of the Ear Nose and Throat Department. He was a true Welshman, and wanted me to stay with him, but I did not fancy spending all my time looking at throats, ears and noses!

A short time after my second post-graduate year I did a locum in Tregaron for Dr Alun Davies, a highly respected doctor in the area. I enjoyed that very much and I still remember how kind the people were. Whenever I visited a farm I was given something to take home – a chicken, eggs, potatoes – reminiscent of the chickens and guinea fowl which the African village chiefs gave me in Ghana. The people in Tregaron had tremendous faith in Dr Alun. This is illustrated by the following true story:

It was a Tuesday in Tregaron, market day, and the town was full of farmers. One farmer came to my surgery and said to me in Welsh, 'I want a bottle for my cough.'

I asked him a lot of questions (there was a lot of tuberculosis around at that time) and then told him to take his coat, waistcoat and shirt off. He looked at me and asked, 'Do you want to examine me?'

'Yes,' I said

I was sorry I had asked him because he took ages to take his clothes off. When I was examining his chest with my stethoscope he said, 'There's a good doctor Dr Alun is. He knows what's wrong with you without an examination.'

That is an example of true faith in the doctor.

Dr Alun knew his patients; he was born and bred in Tregaron. The local people were very honest. They would telephone for medicines or a repeat prescription. 'Put it on the milk lorry,' they would say. The milk lorry was parked overnight in the village ready to start off at dawn to collect the milk churns from the farms. All I had to do was to open the door of the cab and leave the medicines on the seat. No locking of doors – absolute trust. All cough medicines had to be black and have a horrible taste!

I then applied to do one more postgraduate job, this time in Obstetrics, and I was accepted in St David's Hospital, Cardiff, for one year. I was the House Surgeon and my immediate chief was the Senior House Surgeon – a Scots girl, very efficient and very pretty. She was from Edinburgh. How did she come to Cardiff? A new Professor of Obstetrics was appointed to Cardiff. He came from Edinburgh and the Scots girl (Elinor) was his house surgeon there. He asked her whether she would like to go with him to Cardiff as his Senior House Surgeon and she thought this was an excellent idea. She came, and the result was that I married my boss! When we became engaged, I remember, I had very little money and the engagement ring I bought for her was second-hand. Despite this, it was a very nice ring. As a permanent reminder of Professor Duncan, who was instrumental in bringing Elinor and me together, we called one of our four children Duncan.

I completed my Obstetrics course and went to London to sit an examination for the Diploma in Obstetrics and Gynaecology.

I passed and that diploma, which was evidence of practical experience in Obstetrics, was of value to me in my work as a doctor, both in my practice and when I was appointed a Clinical Assistant in Obstetrics and Gynaecology in Bronglais Hospital, Aberystwyth. I worked under the Consultant Obstetrician, Mr Geoffrey Williams. He was a man of few words but he was an expert at his work.

So ended my medical training and I was now ready to embark on my medical career, which extended over the next 32 years.

CHAPTER 7

MEDICAL PRACTICE IN ABERYSTWYTH

After I qualified as a doctor in 1953, and completed my postgraduate training in 1955, it was difficult to obtain a vacancy in general practice. I had an offer of a vacancy in Saundersfoot, which would have been ideal, but unfortunately the doctor I was to replace changed his mind about going to Canada. I then wrote to Dr D.I. Evans in Aberystwyth and asked him if he knew of any vacancies in his area. I was very lucky! His assistant was leaving and Dr Evans offered me the post of 'Assistant with a View' in his practice. The other doctor in the practice was Dr Margaret Morgan, daughter of the founder of the practice. It was usual in those days for an 'Assistant with a View' to wait for three or four years before becoming a full time partner. After one year Dr Evans took me into the practice as a full partner and I remained as such for the next 32 years until I retired on 31 December 1986.

I started work in the practice in June 1955 and Elinor and I were married in September. We lived in a flat for a while and then bought the 'practice house' from Dr Evans, 24 North Parade.

The reader will recall that I had frequent contact with Dr Evans when I was in the Public Health Department and he was the Borough Medical Officer of Health (MOH). Dr Evans was a science graduate and had obtained a PhD. He worked as a Biochemist on a tea plantation in Ceylon (now Sri Lanka). When on leave he met and eventually married Gwen, another daughter of Dr M.J. Morgan, the founder of the practice. He went to Medical School in London at the age of 39 and, on graduation, he took over the practice from his father-in-law.

To practise medicine in Aberystwyth was the height of luxury. The environment was perfect and we had the added advantage of a base hospital in the town. A new District General Hospital of 199 beds was built in 1966. Aberystwyth is a University town and the family doctor is very much a 'Town and Gown' person because of his very frequent contact with students and staff.

Aberystwyth is a seaside resort bordering Cardigan Bay in the County of Ceredigion (previously known as Cardiganshire). It is difficult to assess the present day population but when the Borough was the administrative district the mid-winter population was 11,000. Today the villages outside Aberystwyth have expanded beyond recognition and have become the commuter belts for Aberystwyth. The town has an interesting history. The Borough was established in 1277 when King Edward I granted the town a Charter. The King also built a castle and a small walled town grew around it. The usual practice was to ask a new king to confirm the Charter and this was done by subsequent kings with little amendment 'until 1380 when the Charter of Richard II excluded Welshmen from any part of the civic jurisdiction, common pasture rights and timber and turf rights' ('Aberystwyth Borough, 1277 – 1974' Howard C Jones). The Borough was abolished in 1974 when local government reorganisation declared that the County would be the administrative district. This had to come but the word 'local' lost its meaning for the people of Aberystwyth.

The main industries of 'Old Aberystwyth' were fishing, ship building, agriculture, tourism and lead mining – lead being extensively mined in the hills outside Aberystwyth. The lead was exported from the harbour. In 1874 it is recorded that there were 300 ships registered in the port, but the lead trade ceased in 1930 and the harbour is now a marina – a home for exotic yachts mainly owned by well-heeled individuals from England. Holiday-makers still pour into Aberystwyth in the summer months but they stay, not so much in Aberystwyth, but in the massive caravan parks in the neighbourhood. The visitors increase the work of the family doctors – my practice saw about a thousand visitors every year, mainly in the months of July and August. The castle ruins attract many visitors and the local council carefully maintains the site.

It sometimes rains in Aberystwyth! In the town the annual average is 35 inches per annum. Inland it is much higher. There is a story about an American visitor to Wales. He was complaining to a local resident, 'I don't like Wales. It is always raining here, it is cold here, and you people babble away in Welsh.'

The Cardiganshire man replied, 'Well, sir, next time you go to Hell. It won't be raining there, it will not be cold there, and I can guarantee you that you won't hear any Welsh spoken there.'

The University of Wales in Aberystwyth was founded in 1872. It was then a college by the sea but it is now the college on the hill and in 2001 it has about 7,000 students. It is probably invidious of me to single out departments of excellence but, in this context, I must name the Department of International Politics, the Department of Earth Studies, the Physics Department, and the Law Department (which was 100 years old in 2001).

Aberystwyth is fortunate to have another high-powered centre of learning and research, the National Library of Wales, which is a copyright library. Aberystwyth is also the centre for many Government departments, banks, building societies and, fortunately, a modern hospital.

Despite the increase in official recognition of the Welsh language, Aberystwyth is still mainly English speaking. I am Welsh speaking and I used the language in my practice, probably on a 50/50 basis. I am not in favour of the modern trend towards full bilingualism which has led to much confrontation, due to the unsavoury activities of Welsh language extremists.

An old lady who lived in a rural part of my practice was very deaf. Many times I suggested that she should have a hearing aid but she refused. The deafness got worse and one day she said to me: 'All right, doctor, I will have a hearing aid if it speaks Welsh to me.'

This very brief history of Aberystwyth provides the background to my work in the town from 1955 to 1986. Dr D.I. Evans and Dr Margaret Morgan retired when their time came and, for at least half of my time in practice, I was in partnership with Dr Brian Williams – a first class doctor, never afraid of hard work – and my wife, Elinor, who became an indoor partner when our four children were firmly settled in school. In the early days the surgery was open from 9-10 am and 5-7 pm. The receptionists went home after morning surgery and came back for the evening session. This meant that the surgery was empty for most of the day and, in common with all the other doctors' wives, my wife had to stay in during the day to answer the telephone for emergency calls etc.

Many practices were adopting an appointments system but this was not always satisfactory because patients could not necessarily see the doctor on the day that they needed diagnosis and treatment. The alternative system, which we adopted, was to keep the surgery open all day from 9.00 am to 6.00 pm and the three doctors would do two-hour sessions morning and afternoon. An example of a typical morning would be:

9.00 - 11.00 am	Dr A
10.00 - 12.00 noon	Dr B
11.00 - 1.00 pm	Dr C

The sessions by Dr B overlapped the other Sessions and catered for the busy time. The pattern was repeated in the afternoon with a break between 1.00 and 2.00 pm. This system was particularly well suited to a practice such as ours which had to deal with visitors, about a thousand a year, as already stated. The one disadvantage to the system was that some patients had to wait a long time to see the doctor. One patient waited for over an hour to see me. When she came to my room she said, 'Well, doctor bach, I have waited so long to see you I've forgotten what I came to see you about.'

Generally speaking patients preferred to wait, knowing that they could see the doctor that day, rather than wait a week or so under an appointments system. There is a story about a patient who went to the surgery for an appointment to see the doctor. She went there on a Monday morning and was told by the receptionist that she could see the doctor on the following Friday at 9.00 am. 'That's no good,' she said. 'I'll be better by then.'

The smooth running of a medical practice depends entirely on the receptionist. She has to be diplomatic, courteous and efficient. It is not an easy job but we were fortunate to have a succession of excellent receptionists. Mrs Maureen Kay was superb and was with us for very many years. I am pleased to record that, after my time, the Association of Health Centres and Practice Administrators named her Practice Manager of the Year. She was awarded a prize of £2,000 and £500 for the surgery. I have no doubt that the award was well deserved.

This was a very busy practice but easy to run because the majority of the patients lived in the Aberystwyth area, a radius of about six miles (with the sea on one side!). The requests for home visits were very few. The night calls were about 30 every three months and I can honestly say that the calls at night were genuine emergencies. Sometimes it was only reassurance that was necessary but I must stress this – reassurance is never a waste of time. Our on-call system was simple. I was on call every night for a week and Dr Williams likewise in the following week. Patients would thereby see a doctor they knew when they were ill at night and the doctor had access to the medical notes. I dislike the modern system where doctors form 'co-operatives' to cover night calls, which means that the patient will more often than not see a doctor he does not know and, even worse, the doctor may have no knowledge of the patient's medical history. Nurses who man the telephone have a difficult task and giving advice on the phone is a medico-legal hazard. We have to move with the times but I still prefer our old system!

Our practice grew rapidly over the years and when I retired in 1986 we had just over nine thousand patients on our medical list. Our practice was 'university orientated' and we had a high proportion of students. The majority of our patients were very co-operative and understanding. I nearly always answered their questions truthfully. For many patients the fear of a disease is more difficult to deal with than the disease itself.

In common with a sample of doctors in the UK I took part in a Practice Morbidity Survey. I had to record every aspect of my work for one week and I picked at random the results for week commencing 2 October 1984. Total face-to-face consultations during that week were 347, a daily average over six days of 58. October is always a busy month with the students back in college and this pushes the figures up, but I rarely saw less than 50 people a day. Family doctors deal with 90% of the illness in the community and I will list below a sample of what I saw in my surgery or in the home in one day during the survey week as stated above:

V = *Visit*   S = *Surgery*

V –	Common Cold	S –	Cataract
V –	Post-Natal visit	V –	Flu injection. Heart failure
V –	Pleurisy	V –	Stroke
S –	Leukaemia	V –	Heart Failure
S –	Cystitis	V –	Child with feeding difficulties
S –	Lumbago	S –	Asthma
S –	Fracture of leg	S –	Acute Bronchitis
S –	Early Pregnancy	S –	Tonsillitis
S –	Schizophrenia	S –	Contraception
S –	Polymyalgia	S –	Insomnia
S –	Eczema	S –	Hypertension
S –	Diabetes	S –	Fibrositis
S –	Anxiety State	S –	Pre-senile dementia
S –	Conjunctivitis	S –	Angina
S –	Ingrowing Toe Nail	S –	Obesity
S –	Ears syringed	S –	Anaemia. Investigations
S –	Cancer of breast	S –	Osteoarthritis
S –	Acute appendicitis	S –	Cancer of bowel

I arranged to see the pregnant women and children for immunisation by appointment outside my surgery sessions. There was never a dull moment and never any time to waste. As someone once said, 'If you have time to spare, don't spend it with someone who hasn't.'

It is sometimes said that a doctor can bury his mistakes but this is not true. Every doctor has been faced with the problem of someone dying when, in retrospect, he feels that if he had done something else the outcome would have been different. This is a burden that the doctor has to carry and results from the risk inherent in any medical procedure. No doctor can guarantee that an operation or medication will be successful. The law protects the doctor in this situation provided that what he did, or did not do, was in accordance with what 'a responsible body of medical opinion skilled in that particular art' would have done. A doctor must always do his best for the patient. He has a duty to keep up-to-date and involve the patient in the decision-making process. In the old days it was 'Doctor knows best' but today patient autonomy is the dominant factor.

Hippocrates, the father of medicine, was asked what he said to patients when he prescribed for them. 'I say nothing,' he said. 'If they get better they come back to thank me. If they die they are not there to blame me.' That does not apply today!

Medicine is a science and an art. We learn the science of medicine in college but we learn the art of medicine when faced with the practical problems of dealing with patients who expect doctors to do the best for them. The 'best' may not always be what they want, e.g. a patient asking for antibiotics for a simple cold.

In addition to my day-to-day medical duties I was also a Clinical Assistant in Obstetrics and Gynaecology in Bronglais Hospital. I was on duty from 09.00 hrs on Mondays until 09.00 hrs on Tuesday. I assisted my boss, Mr Geoffrey Williams, at operating sessions on Mondays at 2.00 pm and this often went on until 7.00 pm. This was demanding work and it was not unusual for me to be up all night. The midwives did most of the work but the Clinical Assistant had to attend to the complicated obstetrics – breech delivery, forceps delivery, foetal and maternal distress. It was a happy time because the mothers were so delighted after the event. I gave up this appointment after 20 years because of the dual responsibility of my practice and hospital work.

There is a great deal more I could say about my medical practice, but I will confine my final remarks to four items which may be of general interest.

1 THE CHANGING PATTERN OF DISEASE

Immunisation saw the virtual disappearance of the infectious diseases. It is essential to maintain a level of about 90% of children being immunised to produce 'herd immunity'. The majority of young doctors today have not seen cases of diphtheria, smallpox or poliomyelitis. These diseases used to kill or maim children and adults but have now disappeared. However, doctors have to be on guard.

In the last two years of the 20th century the immunisation rate in the UK declined because mothers were not happy with the MMR vaccine (combined measles, mumps and rubella). It has been reported in the medical press that there could be a connection between this particular vaccine and autism. The Republic of Ireland is suffering its worse measles epidemic for many years because the concern about the MMR vaccine has meant the uptake of this vaccine is only 76% (*British Medical Journal*). Mothers asking for the measles vaccine to be given alone can't get it in the UK but it is freely available in France. Diphtheria is appearing again in Russia, severe life-threatening measles in the Balkans, and poliomyelitis is always in the Third World.

The young mothers of today have not seen these diseases and have become complacent, which is very dangerous. Sometimes a mother would ask me if the 'immunisation' was safe when we were concerned about the whooping cough vaccine. My reply satisfied them: 'I have given the injection to my own children.'

2 THE USE AND ABUSE OF ANTIBIOTICS

The era of antibiotics started in 1928 when Fleming discovered Penicillin, but this drug was not really processed until 1945. Two

A name so close to my heart that even a signpost generates emotion . . .

Pistyll at Cwmbychanmawr, Commins Coch
'The other adventure, which is ingrained in my mind, is that to wash
in the morning we went outside to the yard with a bar of red
Lifebuoy soap and washed under the *pistyll . . .*'

Pistyll in rural
Cardiganshire.
Picture: Mr Terry Bromley

The refurbished fireplace at Tycerrig showing the open door of the wall oven, the 'ffwrn wal'.

'A fire was lit inside the oven using good quality wood, usually oak. After a while, most of the ashes were removed but some were pushed to the sides of the oven. The large bread tins were then put in the oven and, after a suitable interval, were taken out and replaced by a huge fruit cake and smaller cakes. One baking a week was the usual pattern.'

The author's children: Andrew, Jonathan, Duncan and Kathryn.
The photograph was taken in the garden
of their home in Aberystwyth in 1966.

The children in 2001: Kathryn, Andrew, Duncan and Jonathan.
The photograph was taken at a party to celebrate my mother-in-law's
97th birthday in September 2000.

'Friday night was free and in the winter our major hobby was rug making. The wool was not "ready-cut" in those days – we had to cut it ourselves. We made many rugs and some are in use in my house today or by the beds of our grandchildren.'

Rug-making: a passion in youth and in later life.

Commins Coch Post Office – an annexe to the main house.
'The post-office was established towards the end of the 19th century and my grandfather was probably the first postmaster. The post-office remained in the family until my mother retired in the early 1960's.'

Hafod, the author's house in Commins Coch.
'My parents decided to build a modern semi-bungalow on one of our fields with a small shop to accommodate the village post office.'

The reopening of the renovated chapel.
Such a publication now seems a relic of a bygone age
and of a community that seems so very far away.
'The chapel is still there but there has been a steady decline in membership over the past 25 years and in recent years there has been only one Sunday service with no resident minister and no Sunday School. On Sunday 26 November 2000 the chapel closed for the winter. Will it reopen? I doubt it.'

Commins Coch Council School, circa 1926.
John Hughes kneels third from the right in the front row.

Hughes, J.H. RAMC, 1942 – 47

'19.1.46: Received the best news of the war – the award of the British Empire Medal – BEM (Mil.) for my work in Wa during the epidemic of meningitis. It appears that my name appeared in the New Year Honours List 1946.'

Part of the roof of a Dagarti house. This house, not a particularly large one, houses over 100 people. The above is typical of the houses in the Wa area. The people on the left are standing on the roof of the house.

Reprinted from the *Journal of Tropical Medicine and Hygiene.* Aug/Sept 1957 by kind permission of the Editor. From an article by Dr B.B. Waddy, 'African Epidemic Cerebro-Spinal Meningitis.'

My friend in war and peace, Peter Kinton, also RAMC.
In civilian life Peter became Chief Environmental Health Officer for
Kingston, Surrey. The photo was taken at the Red Kite Centre near
Aberystwyth, June 2000.

John Hughes (right) presenting the report on the Meningitis outbreak to
Mr P. H. Starling, Curator of the RAMC Museum. 28 June 2000.

The author and his wife, Elinor, at the site of the first recognised Medical School (Hippocrates) on the island of Kos in Greece.

'I qualified as a doctor in 1953. My first post-graduate appointment was as House Physician in Paediatrics under Professor Watkins. I worked for six months in the Royal Infirmary in Cardiff and six months in Llandough Hospital . . .

My pay for the first six months was £50 and £100 for the second six months, plus food. In my second post-graduate year I was appointed House Surgeon to Mr Hugh Jones.'

*John and Elinor married on 17th September 1955
at Braid Church, Edinburgh.*

'My immediate chief was the Senior House Surgeon – a Scots girl,
very efficient and very pretty. She was from Edinburgh.
How did she come to Cardiff? A new Professor of Obstetrics was
appointed to Cardiff. He came from Edinburgh and the Scots girl
(Elinor) was his house surgeon there. He asked her whether she
would like to go with him to Cardiff as his Senior House Surgeon
and she thought this was an excellent idea. She came, and the result
was that I married my boss!'

The 'practice house' in Aberystwyth, 24 North Parade.

A 'town and gown' practice in Aberystwyth.
For 32 years students, tourists and locals all demand the Doctor's skills.

The author in his surgery on the last day in medical practice, 31 December 1986.

Photo: Rolant Ellis

Daffodils at Sŵn-y-Nant, Commins Coch.
The result of many years of enjoyable planting.

Tea on the lawn with Dr and Mrs Loyn.
Sŵn-y–Nant, Commins Coch, 1991.

of Britain's top scientists, Ernest Chain and Howard Florey, took the drug to America in 1938-39 and worked on it during the war. They, and Fleming, were awarded the Nobel Prize. M and B 693 was available before the war but this was mainly a bacteriostatic – it stopped bacteria growing so that the patient's own immune system could deal with the infection. However, it gave rise to the family of sulphonamides of which one, Sulphanilamide, proved invaluable in the outbreak of meningitis in Ghana (see Chapter 5).

Patients came to expect, and sometimes demand, antibiotics for any minor ailment and some doctors found that it was easier to prescribe than to argue. Bacteria are not daft, they want to survive as well, and sooner or later they develop a resistance to the drug.

Doctors today are faced with a very dangerous situation which concerns one bacteria in particular – Methicillin Resistant Staphylococcus Aureus (MRSA). This is a 'pus forming' organism, usually on the skin, and often proves fatal when it invades the blood stream. This germ lurks in many of our hospitals today and is a classical example of the dangers that lie ahead if doctors continue to prescribe antibiotics when all that is required is explanation and reassurance.

Another hazard is the widespread use of antibiotics in animals to encourage growth. In my opinion this is wrong and should be banned.

It is not easy to send a patient away without a prescription but, as Dr William Evans, a distinguished Welsh physician, once said, 'It is better to do nothing when nothing is indicated than doing something when nothing is indicated.' Very true but difficult. Patients have tremendous faith in antibiotics.

A man came out of hospital after having an 'open and close' operation. There was nothing that could be done for him and he knew this. The vicar called to see him and after hearing the sad story he said, 'I am very sorry about this. I will put you on the prayer list in the Church.'

'There is no need,' said the man. 'I'm on antibiotics.'

3 DRUG TAKING IN THE COMMUNITY

Drug taking is an example of the great change in medical practice in my time as a family doctor. At one time all my patients were happy with a 'bottle', either for a cough, stomach, bowels or as a tonic. Then came the age of the tranquillisers and sleeping tablets. At first the sleeping tablets were phenobarbitones. There were many suicides from overdosage and doctors were told to change to Mandrax. This was an excellent sleeping tablet but it quickly became a drug of addiction. Then came Mogadon which is still in use. The tranquillisers, e.g. Valium and Librium, were widely used, also the stimulant drug Drinamyl, which was an amphetamine drug. Many patients became dependent on these drugs, a lot due to 'repeat prescriptions' obtained by merely telephoning the surgery. The patient might not be seen for months unless he or she (usually a she) had some other complaint. This also applied to other medications, such as drugs for heart failure and, in particular, the anti-arthritic drugs, Brufen and Nurofen, and many other non-steroidal anti-inflammatory drugs (NSAIDs). Doctors were alerted in March 2000 when a report in the journal *Pain* said, 'Pain relieving drugs including the NSAIDs are killing thousands of people each year . . . the hidden cost of long term medication.'

Doctors were advised to, 'ensure that patients are given the lowest doses for the shortest possible time.' It is very difficult to wean patients off tablets which have become part of their way of life, but this has to be done, despite much unpleasantness. Patients today must get out of the habit of drug taking and doctors are obliged to prescribe for short periods and then review.

In a lecture I gave in Jerusalem to an International Symposium on Drug Abuse (1972) I said:

> Children learn by example. If they are given tablets and medicines in childhood they will expect something similar when they face the problems of adolescent life. Children today see their parents taking tablets and medicines for various ailments first thing in the morning, before and after meals, and again at night. The tablets are on the table

alongside the sugar basin. The children look upon this as normal and this idea is reinforced by mother's frequent visits to the doctor. This early introduction to drugs is reflected in the adolescent age group when the young person goes to college or even earlier. Anxiety about work and fears of sexual inadequacy added to a basic personality weakness renders the student at risk for alcohol, drugs, or even suicide.

I am quite certain that doctors have, unwittingly, been guilty of starting people on the road to drug dependence. It is not the drug that is at fault but the drug taker. Heroin is a drug of addiction yet family and hospital doctors use heroin and its analogues extensively. As John Hunter, a famous physician and anatomist, said in 1797, 'The Almighty would have fallen far short of his acknowledged mercy if He had not furnished us with opium when he gave us pain.' If a mother or father needs to take any medication this should take place in private and not in front of the children. Let us all remember the old aphorism which is still very true today, 'Drugs cure the sick but make the healthy ill.'

4 THE ABUSE OF ALCOHOL

Alcohol has been around for a very long time. There are many references to it in the Bible. In St. Paul's first letter to Timothy (5.23) the recommendation is, 'Drink no longer water, but use a little wine for thy stomach's sake and thine often infirmities.' Then there is also that warning from Proverbs (23.31-32), 'Don't let wine tempt you . . . the next morning you will feel as if you had been bitten by a poisonous snake.' And verse 33 in the same chapter could be taken as a reference to the present day office party, 'Thine eyes shall behold strange women, and thine heart shall utter perverse things.'

Alcohol is socially acceptable but it can become a drug of addiction. When this happens it ruins the victim as well as his family. The vandalism which is common today is often alcohol related. If a person really wants to stop drinking he can do so.

When this is suggested to him he may well say: 'I can carry my drink. It does not affect me at all.'

People will never admit to drinking too much, but spending a lot of money on drink leads to wife beating and child poverty. When such a person becomes an established alcoholic there is no cure – he is merely in remission until the next drink.

There is the story of a man who had a terrible time with his wife and to help him cope he spent most evenings in the pub and ultimately became an alcoholic. His wife went to her doctor to ask for help.

'You must cure him, doctor,' she said.

The doctor suggested various ways in which he could be helped.

'I've tried all that,' she said, 'all useless.'

'You must now think of some way of giving him a shock,' said the doctor.

'I will try that,' she said.

One moonlit night she dressed up as the Devil and hid behind a gravestone in the cemetery. She knew that her husband always came home through the cemetery. When he approached she jumped out in front of him.

'Who are you?' he said.

'I'm the Devil,' she replied.

'Well, well,' he said, 'I'm very pleased to meet you. I married your sister.'

There is another story concerning a doctor who went to a school to teach children about the danger of alcohol. He put two glasses on the table in front of him. Into one glass he put water. Into the other glass he put gin. He then put a worm in each. The worm in the water moved about happily. The worm in the gin fell motionless to the bottom of the glass. The doctor then asked the class, 'What do you learn from that?'

One boy put his hand up and said, 'Please Sir, if you have worms, drink gin.'

The alcoholic is a most difficult patient to treat. He is a

conman and a first class liar. He will agree with everything you suggest in the surgery and then go to the pub on the way home. These people do better in specialised alcoholic units being 'dried out' and rehabilitated. They need then to obey the 'all or none' law because the first drink can put them back to square one.

One consolation. Alcohol in moderate amounts is a pleasant drink and helps blood flow in arteries and, as such, is beneficial in angina and as a preventative of strokes. The best time to take it is at night (provided you are not taking sleeping tablets). There is some evidence that red wine is the most beneficial but whisky is my favourite, and a good general rule is a double whisky for the husband and a single one for his wife.

CHAPTER 8

ABORTION AND THE UNIVERSITY OF WALES, ABERYSTWYTH

In my early days as a house surgeon in Llandough Hospital, Cardiff, I had to be on emergency duty on certain days of the week. I well remember the women who came in bleeding and collapsed after 'back-street' abortions. They were very ill and a major problem for the young doctor because they would need an urgent blood transfusion and the veins needed to administer this would have collapsed. That was in 1954. We had to wait until 1967 for the Abortion Act, which was a major advance in humanitarian medicine. The Act proclaimed that an abortion would not be unlawful if two doctors, acting in good faith, were of the opinion 'that continuance of the pregnancy would involve risk to the life of the pregnant woman greater than if the pregnancy were terminated.'

Long before the Abortion Act 1967 the word 'life' had been interpreted not necessarily as death, but as the physical and mental health of the patient during her life (R v Bourne, 1939). This opinion was controversial at the time but the principle was incorporated in the 1967 Act, which states that, when deciding the issue, 'account may be taken of the woman's actual or reasonable foreseeable environment.' An example might be a student in college, or a young schoolgirl, or a woman in her 40's who was 'family complete'. Abortion on demand was not the will of Parliament but abortion on request is surely desirable.

I found the Abortion Act of immense value and help in my practice. Before the Act it was sometimes necessary to have the advice of a psychiatrist before a girl could have an abortion. What nonsense. 'Abortion' is an emotive word and, as a rule, I prefer to use the term 'termination of pregnancy'.

The Abortion Act is constantly under threat and attempts have been made on at least fourteen occasions in Parliament to amend it in a restrictive way. Fortunately, they all failed, except for an amendment that made abortion unlawful after 24 weeks (down from 28 weeks) unless there were *substantial* risks to the health of the mother and the effects on any existing children of the family. I firmly believe that whether a woman has her pregnancy terminated should not be a doctor's choice but should be her choice. It is her body and, as I have said in the past, if men could have babies we would have had an Abortion Act long before 1967. Some doctors refuse termination of pregnancy on moral grounds. The law allows them to opt out but ethically they should refer the patient to another doctor who may have a different view. Delay is dangerous. A termination before twelve weeks is safe but at eight weeks it is both safe and simple. This means that the earlier the patient comes to the doctor the better.

But not as early as one patient of mine who telephoned me at 2 am saying that she was very worried because she could be pregnant. I told her to come to see me in the morning so that we could discuss the matter. I then asked her, 'How far on are you?'

'Five minutes,' she said.

I am sure that many women can sympathise with her!

In the period 1966-68 there was a considerable increase in the number of students entering the University. The University decided that there should be some form of Student Health Service. One General Practitioner in the town, Dr Elwyn Hughes, was appointed to deal with the students who had declared that they had a medical problem, and I was appointed to run a counselling service. Both appointments were part-time. Some of the students who came to me were very unhappy and presented with a variety of problems – homesickness, failure to adapt to the new environment, anxiety about work, insomnia and sexual problems. Some wanted contraceptive advice but the Principal (Dr Thomas Parry, later Sir Thomas) refused to allow me to provide this. One student became pregnant. She told her tutor and in due course the facts became known to the Principal. He declared that she should not be seen on campus during her pregnancy, which meant she could not attend lectures. I objected to this but the Principal's word was the law.

In 1968 I was invited to read a paper at an international congress in London on 'Contraception in the University'. In this paper I referred to the importance of free contraceptive advice and went on to say:

> . . . the pregnancy rate in Aberystwyth is well below the national average but I still consider it to be much too high. It means that 10 to 15 students are pregnant at probably the most important time of their lives, some in their first year and some just before the final examinations – a tragedy for the individual and a major catastrophe for the parents.

I then referred to the Abortion Act 1967 and how valuable it was because it would help 'doctors to deal with the pregnant student.'

I sent a copy of the lecture to the Registrar of the college and in a covering letter I said how pleased I was that the Abortion Act had enabled me to arrange an abortion for ten students during that academic year. The Registrar passed my proposed lecture and the covering letter to the Principal. When the Principal read my lecture and the covering letter, war broke out! I received a letter from him the very next morning – see *Letter No. 1*, dated 23 January 1968.

I replied by return of post and *Letter No. 2*, dated 24 January 1968, is a carbon copy of my reply. Looking back at this 32 years later I gave the correct answer despite very limited knowledge of medical ethics at that time.

The Principal replied and the war was now firmly declared! – *Letter No. 3*, 26 January 1968. I replied by return of post – *Letter No. 4*, 27 January 1968. The Principal called for my resignation –

COLEG PRIFYSGOL CYMRU
UNIVERSITY COLLEGE OF WALES

LETTER
No 1

Prifathro
Principal
THOMAS PARRY, D.Litt., F.B.A.

CONFIDENTIAL

ABERYSTWYTH.
TELEPHONE N°? 2711

23rd January, 1968

Dear Dr. Hughes,

The Registrar has shown me your letter to him and the summary of the paper which you propose to give at the International Congress on Mental Health in August.

I note that there were 10 cases of pregnancy among students of this College last session. Will you please let me have a list of the names of the women concerned with brief case-histories (marked 'confidential') ?

I shall then want to discuss with you and Dr. Elwyn Hughes the function of the Student Health Service in respect of this and other matters.

Yours sincerely,

Thomas Parry.

Dr. John H. Hughes,
24 North Parade,
Aberystwyth

LETTER NO 2.

Copy:

24.1.68.

Dear Dr Thomas Parry,

Thank you very much for your letter regarding pregnancy in the College.

I am afraid I cannot give you the information you request. The strict ethical code prevents me from giving information of this nature to any third party.

I am sure you will realise that my work as a doctor would be impossible if the student (i.e. the patient) suspected any breach of faith of this nature.

I will certainly see you at any time to discuss the general problem.

Yours sincerely,

John H Hughes.

LETTER No 3

Prifysgol Cymru University of Wales.

Vice-Chancellor:
Thomas Parry, M.A., D.Litt., F.B.A.

University College of Wales
Aberystwyth
(Telephone : 2711)

CONFIDENTIAL

26th January, 1968

Dear Dr. Hughes,

Thank you for your letter of 24th January.

I was very surprised to find that you are unwilling to let me have a list of women students who became pregnant during last session. Do you mean to say that I as Principal of this College am not entitled to this information ? As a matter of fact all members of the Senate and the Council could well claim that they should be told something about the situation, but I don't intend to pass the information on to anybody.

Your relationship with students is not that of the ordinary general practitioner, but rather that of a College Medical Officer, and, therefore, the "strict ethical code" which you mention must be modified to the slight degree that is envisaged in my request.

You must realize that I as Principal must not be kept in ignorance of the pregnancy issue. I would be failing in my duty if I did not take steps to inform myself fully of the state of affairs, including the names of all affected persons. If I were asked a question by a member of Senate or of the Council, or by a parent, how do you think I would be regarded if I were to say that all I knew was that there were ten cases of pregnancy in the College ? As I suggested in my previous letter, I am prepared to treat the facts as strictly confidential.

I must insist on your giving me the information I asked for. If you refuse, I shall have no option but to refer the whole issue to the College Council, and this, as you can well imagine, would bring things to a very undesirable pass.

I want this information, and I want it immediately, please.

Yours sincerely,

Dr. John H. Hughes,
24 North Parade,
Aberystwyth

COPY   **Letter No 4**

Dr Margaret I Morgan   24 North Parade,
Dr John H Hughes   Aberystwyth.

                                        27th January 1968

Dear Dr Parry,

    Thank you for your further letter re pregnancy in College students.

    The fact that you are Principal of the College and that I am Medical Officer makes not the slightest difference to the position which I stated in my last letter.

    I will not comment further at this stage but will gladly address the College Council and/or the Senate if invited to do so.

    Yours sincerely,

(John H Hughes)

Dr Thomas Parry,
Principal,
U.C.W., Aberystwyth.

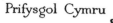 University of Wales.

Prifysgol Cymru

LETTER No 5

Vice-Chancellor:
Thomas Parry, M.A., D.Litt., F.B.A.

CONFIDENTIAL

University College of Wales
Aberystwyth
(Telephone : 2711)

31 January, 1968

Dear Dr. Hughes,

I had a talk with the President last night about the matter which was discussed by you and Dr. Elwyn Hughes and myself yesterday morning.

The President's views on the relationship between a Student Health Officer and the Principal are identical with mine, and he instructed me to ask for your resignation, which, with deep regret, I am now doing. I leave it to you to indicate the date on which your resignation would become operative. It might be the end of the present term, or earlier, if you think it more appropriate.

Yours sincerely,

Thomas Parry.

Dr. John Hughes,
24 North Parade,
Aberystwyth

Prifysgol Cymru University of Wales.

Vice-Chancellor:
Thomas Parry, M.A., D.Litt., F.B.A.

CONFIDENTIAL

University College of Wales
Aberystwyth
(Telephone : 2711)

5th February, 1968

Dear Dr. Hughes,

     I have received your letter of 3rd February and the copy of the letter from the Medical Defence Union.

     I note that the Secretary speaks of "your professional duties," and "your professional attendance." These phrases might refer to your private practice as a general practitioner, in which case they would, of course, be right and proper. There is nothing in the letter to indicate that they refer to you in the capacity of Student Health Officer.

     Be that as it may, I am still of the opinion that I am fully justified in asking you for full information about pregnant women students, and whatever the Medical Defence Union may think, and in spite of what is said in A Handbook on Student Health Services, I must adhere to that opinion. In this I am firmly reinforced by the very definite ruling of the President of the College, and, therefore, I have no choice but to ask again for your resignation.

          Yours sincerely,

          Thomas Parry.

Dr. John H. Hughes,
24 North Parade,
Aberystwyth

COLEG PRIFYSGOL CYMRU
UNIVERSITY COLLEGE OF WALES

Letter No 1

Prifathro
Principal
THOMAS PARRY, D.Litt., F.B.A.

CONFIDENTIAL

ABERYSTWYTH.

Telephone Nos ⟨XXXXXX⟩ 2711

13th February, 1968

Dear Dr. Hughes,

Since I last wrote to you two things have happened.

(1) I have had a discussion with the Wardens of women students, and I was amazed to find that they are not informed immediately of cases of pregnancy in their own halls. A Warden is in a particularly advantageous position to be able to help in such cases. The Wardens are naturally dissatisfied with the present state of affairs.

(2) I consulted the Officers of the College last evening, and they were definitely of the view that my attitude in this matter is perfectly reasonable, and that it is the only attitude I could adopt without failing in my duty as Principal of the College.

Having taken this advice, and having given the matter a considerable amount of very serious thought, I am prepared to withdraw my request for your resignation if you will agree to observe the following conditions in future :

(a) That I be given, in strict confidence, the name of any pregnant woman living in lodgings or in a flat.

(b) That you inform me, again in the strictest confidence, what treatment is proposed for her.

(c) That the Warden be informed immediately if a case of pregnancy occurs in a hall of residence.

I am not now asking you for any comments on the ten cases of pregnancy that occurred here last session; nor am I asking you to tell me anything about a pregnant woman except the above simple facts.

Dr. John Hughes,
24 North Parade,
Aberystwyth

Continued
Next Page

CONFIDENTIAL

LETTER No 7

Dr. John Hughes   13th February, 1968

     I would emphasize that the information I am asking for is not meant to be used for any disciplinary or punitive purposes. I would not interview the girl concerned unless there was some special difficulty, and I was asked to do so, and I need hardly add that I would never divulge names to any College body, or indeed to any individual.

     In addition to the point I have already made, namely, that I have a right to this information, there is the further very important point that only the Wardens and I are in a position to make the necessary adjustments in order that pregnancy interferes as little as possible with the girl's academic prospects.

     I shall be very pleased to discuss the matter further with you if you think that would help.

Yours sincerely,

Somerbarry.

Principal

Letter No. 5, 31 January 1968. I thought the time had come for me to consult my medico-legal advisers and I sent a file on the controversy to legal advisors in London. I received a prompt and encouraging reply on 1 February 1968. I was told that I was fully justified in refusing to give the Principal the information he requested, and the ethical position was re-emphasised, namely, that if I had given this information to the Principal, I 'would have transgressed the rule of professional secrecy'.

I wrote to the Principal and sent him a copy of the letter from the legal advisors. I added the following:

> As you can see I was correct in my interpretation of the situation. I have no desire to force an issue but I like my work in the college and I am proud of the fact I am able to help so many students. Do you still want me to resign? (Letter dated 3 February 1968)

A few days later the Principal replied – *Letter No. 6,* 5 February 1968. The Principal referred to 'A Handbook of Student Health Services'. This is what the handbook said with reference to the duties of Student Medical Officers:

> . . . he [the doctor] is the student's doctor, not the college's. Everything told in consultation is a professional confidence and nothing whatsoever can be disclosed without the willing consent of the student. This confidentiality is the bedrock of a successful service.

In one of my interviews with the Principal, he told me I was writing my notes on college paper and that he had a right to have the papers. I replied that the college did indeed own the paper but once I had written medical notes on the paper it became my property.

Two other matters concerned me at the time. The Principal told me that my resignation would be kept quiet and that there would be no minute to record it! Secondly, the Principal told me that the college had drawn up a plan to replace me with a non-medical counsellor. I pointed out that the students would not be happy with that because the new appointee would not be subject to the strict ethical rules of the medical profession.

The Principal wrote to me again – *Letter No. 7* dated 13 February 1968. I obviously could not agree to the requests made, and I was duly sacked on 22 July.

A few weeks later, in August, I was called to a meeting of my advisers in London. High-ranking lawyers, doctors, and doctors from the Student Health Service attended the meeting. The dispute was considered in detail and it was decided that this affair should come into the public domain so as to establish the legal and ethical situation once and for all. To my great surprise the plan was to give the file to Nicholas Lloyd, a top journalist with *The Sunday Times*. A few days later, in August 1968, an article entitled 'Doctor: I was sacked for keeping code' appeared in that newspaper. This was a well-balanced summary of the situation and referred to the fact that the Executive Committee of The Medico-Legal advisers 'consisting of 17 distinguished doctors, gave their whole-hearted support to Dr Hughes' but 'after permission had been given for the controversial lecture to be delivered, the Principal sacked Dr Hughes.'

Next day, the story was in all the national newspapers. An article in the *Daily Express* on 20 August explained the situation and is reproduced at the end of this chapter together with a response from the students published in the *Liverpool Daily Post*. I had letters of support from all over the world, including one from Mr Jack Straw, President of the National Union of Students, the future MP and Secretary of State for Foreign Affairs. The complete file on this episode, plus many of the letters received, will be deposited at the National Library of Wales when I have 'crossed the River Jordan'.

The end of the story is that I was reinstated. I was sacked in the summer and reinstated in the autumn. Much to the surprise of the Principal I was appointed to the Court of Governors of the college! Even more ironical is that, many years later, I was appointed Hon. Lecturer in Medical Law in the Law Department of the University in Aberystwyth.

Dr Thomas Parry was courteous but strict. He thought that he was in Loco Parentis but the Law Department, when asked, ruled that he was not. The lesson we learnt is basic. Confidentiality between doctors and patients is the foundation of a medical practice and must be preserved at all costs and at all times. For my part I agree with John Barrymore (1882-1942) who said, 'The thing that takes up the least amount of time and causes the most amount of trouble is sex.'

Doctor: I was sacked for keeping code

(¹)

By Nicholas Lloyd
Education Correspondent

A ROW has broken out over the sacking of one of the University College of Aberystwyth's student health officers, who claims he has been dismissed for sticking to the doctor's code of professional secrecy and refusing to divulge the names of pregnant girl students.

But the College principal, Dr Thomas Parry, says that he dismissed Dr John Hughes and a fellow part-time student health officer because it became obvious that a full-time and—judging by the salary offered. non-medical —student counsellor was needed.

The Medical Defence Union, which supports Dr Hughes, fears that a student counsellor might give confidential information to the university authorities, although they have no right to medical information a b o u t patients aged 16 or over without the student's permission.

Because of this, although the principal calls it "damn bad form," the M D U has made available to the Sunday Times all the correspondence in its possession concerning the case.

The events culminating in Dr. Hughes' dismissal began in January this year when he asked the college registrar to deliver a paper, "Contraception in the Universities," at last week's Seventh International Congress on Mental Health in London.

Advice for all

In a summary paper which Dr. Hughes presented to the registrar he pointed out that there had been 10 known pregnancies among girls at Aberystwyth in 1967, a pregnancy ratio of 1.5 per cent., well below the national average. He argued that there should be contraceptive advice for all students.

On January 23 the principal wrote to Dr Hughes asking for the names of the 10 pregnant case histories "marked confidential." He added that he would like to discuss with the two doctors the function of the Student Health Service in respect of this and other matters.

Dr Hughes replied that he could not give the information required. The strict ethical code prevented him from giving information of this nature to any third party. His work as a doctor would be impossible if the student (i e, the patient) suspected any breach of faith of this nature, he added.

The principal wrote back asking whether Dr Hughes actually meant to say that he, as principal of the college, was not entitled to information about the pregnant girls. He suggested that Dr Hughes's relationship with the students was not that of ordinary practitioner, but rather of college medical officer, and that therefore the "strict ethical code" must be modified. He again added that he would treat the facts as strictly confidential.

At the end of January the principal asked for Dr Hughes's resignation. But Dr Hughes wrote back saying that he had already contacted the Medical Defence Union who had assured him he was ethically and legally right.

The principal refused to change his attitude, saying he was amazed to find that wardens of the women students' halls of residence had not been informed of the pregnancies, and that the officers of the college were behind him.

He was willing to withdraw the resignation demand on three conditions: that he should be given, in strict confidence, the name of any pregnant woman living in lodgings or in a flat; that Dr Hughes should inform him what treatment was proposed; and that wardens should be informed immediately of a pregnancy in a hall of residence.

He emphasised that the information he was asking for was not meant to be used for any disciplinary or punitive purposes.

Dr Hughes was advised by the M D U to ask the principal why he needed to know the names of pregnant women living in flats and lodgings, and why, although a warden might be able to help, she should be told without the patient's consent.

On March 8 the M D U's executive committee, consisting of 17 distinguished doctors, gave their whole-hearted support to Dr Hughes. Pressure was then exerted by influential academics and doctors on the principal and the affair subsided.

By June 5 Dr Hughes thought the matter had been dropped. But on July 22, after permission had been given for the controversial lecture so long as it was emphasised that it was the doctor's own personal opinion, the principal sacked Dr Hughes and his colleague.

The principal says: "There is absolutely no connection between the discussion I had with Dr John Hughes earlier in the year about pregnant girls and the decision to replace the doctors with a full-time counselling service. The two things are utterly different and i n d e p e n d e n t issues."

He refused yesterday to say precisely why the college decided to replace the doctors. "I am not prepared, like the Medical Defence Union, to blab out private matters in newspapers, however reputable," he said. "The decision was made by a committee because we thought a counselling service would be better. The students themselves were highly dissatisfied with the previous state of affairs and wanted more help and guidance."

Dr Hughes denied yesterday that the students did no other service. He said: "There was a case about 12 months ago of a girl who became pregnant and went to her tutor and told him. The tutor informed the principal and the girl was actually expelled.

"I and some others interceded on the girl's behalf and she was reinstated, but it all caused a terrible fuss at a very worrying time for the girl. For a period her grant was cut off and she had to have National Assistance."

Dr Addison, secretary of the M D U, commented: "Unfortunately, there is nothing further we can do for Dr Hughes. Dr Parry is Vice-Chancellor of the University of Wales as well as principal at Aberystwyth, so there is no one to appeal to. We have simply told Dr Hughes not to pass on his files on patients to any non-medical counsellor."

THE CASE OF TEN PREGNANT GIRLS...

I agree: Doctors should not tell?

DAILY EXPRESS 20:8:68

by TIM HEALD

AT FIRST glance the curious story of University College, Aberystwyth, appears to concern no one but a don, a doctor, and 10 supposedly pregnant girls.

On closer inspection it raises questions of some significance for us all.

These concern the erosion of our private lives, and official interference in what is not officialdom's business.

What's more, they raise some doubts about the possible pressures society can put upon the integrity of our doctors.

Ethics

THE STORY so far is this:—
Ten girls in the college become pregnant. The college medical officer, Dr. John Hughes, reveals the fact after a university conference. The college principal, Dr. Thomas Parry, asks him to give the girls' names if he knows them. Dr. Hughes is asked . . . Dr. Parry says the asking has nothing to do with Dr. Hughes's refusal.

There are two issues involved

here. The first is one of medical ethics.

Did Dr. Hughes have any obligation to reveal the names? The answer seems to be a definite "No." The B.M.A. and the Medical Defence Union both support Dr. Hughes.

The second point is: Did Dr. Parry have any right to ask for the girls' names?

So far he has said that he did not want the names for punitive purposes. If not, then why did he want them? Curiosity? Dr. Parry was evidently taking an interest in the non-academic affairs of his students.

Now, a healthy, helpful interest is one thing; self-righteous interference is quite another.

I am certainly in no position to suggest what Dr. Parry's motives

were. But, there are people in the universities and outside who believe that universities are responsible for more than their pupils' academic affairs.

At Oxford, where I studied for three years, the principal concern was that we should all learn enough to obtain honours degrees. For this purpose we were all allotted tutors.

We were also given a "moral tutor," who was responsible for our moral welfare.

My old moral tutor, an authority on the French Revolution, called Richard Cobb, is currently in South Africa on an exchange fellowship. There he said in an interview that "parents make unreasonable demands on universities.

"Students should be treated as adults," he said and added: "It is not the job of university teachers to go round pulling girls out of men students' beds."

Too many people thought universities were obliged to take on the role of parents' while the students were there.

Taxpayers

THIS, I can say, is not so. Any responsibility is purely moral, and only applies in respect of "reasonable demands.

There is another question which many taxpayers put.

Why should I pay for young people to take drugs, have sex,

drink? The answer to that is that you are paying for them to be given a degree or equivalent with social behaviour differs with their studies then it is of concern. If they work hard then you should be duly grateful.

That with due humility is also my advice to Dr. Parry. Make sure your students do the work required. If they get pregnant in their spare time that is their business. Not yours or the college's.

Parallels

SOME PEOPLE would suggest there are parallels in the Aberystwyth case with any number of business and insurance doctors.

No doubt there have been cases which doctors have passed on information about patients; but the B.M.A. insists that the rule remains the same.

Under no circumstances may information be given to a third party without the patient's permission—although such a patient's mere presence at such a consultation is usually taken as tacit acceptance that some information will be passed on.

No one, but no one, has the right to expect a doctor to give information about a patient without his permission. Now, a doctor has a right to give it. Your health is part of your own private life.

And your private life is nobody else's business.

BOYCOTT THREAT BY STUDENTS

If the University College of Wales, Aberystwyth, appointed a man who was not a qualified doctor the students there would boycott whoever was selected.

This was said last night by Mr Nic Partos, president of the Students' Union at Aberystwyth, commenting on a statement in yesterday's *Daily Post* by Mr Eifion Lloyd Jones, acting general secretary of the Union of Students in Wales on the dismissal of Dr John Hughes as part-time medical attendant at the college.

Mr Partos said he was making known the feelings of the students at Aberystwyth because they did not belong to the U.S.W. who had no right to claim that they were speaking on their behalf.

"We belong to the National Union of Students," Mr Partos said, "and shall continue to do so."

Mr Partos said Dr Hughes was a most popular man at the college and the students did not accept the explanation that Dr Hughes' appointment had been terminated because it had been decided to appoint a full-time non-professional counsellor.

They were convinced that it was due entirely to Dr Hughes' refusal to break his ethical code and give the Principal the names of girl students who had been found to be pregnant.

Want fully qualified man

"As president of the Aberystwyth students," Mr Partos said last night, "I have been invited to the meeting which will choose Dr Hughes' successor.

"It is my intention at that meeting to say that if a man who is not a qualified M.D. is chosen, the students at Aberystwyth will boycott him.

"We are determined to have a fully qualified medical man to look after our interests, someone who will be bound by a medical man's ethical code and not someone whose first responsibility will be to the university authorities."

Liverpool Daily Post, Saturday, August 24, 1968
Reproduced with the permission of the Editor of the *Daily Post*

CHAPTER 9

BROADCASTING

The day after the *Sunday Times* published the article on the Abortion dispute in Aberystwyth my telephone never ceased to ring. I think every national newspaper telephoned me for a comment. English and Welsh radio wanted an interview and, of course, television.

All this was very sudden and quite new to me. I had to rush to the dictionary to find Welsh words for abortion (*erthyliad*) and contraception (*atal cenhedlu*) and the interviews went on for about a week. I was receiving letters and telephone calls from all over the world, many of them from old patients of mine.

This major exposure to the media led to a lifetime of broadcasting. I can look back on taking part in studio programmes in Cardiff and Bangor with such high-ranking personalities as Vincent Kane, Gwilym Owen, Vaughan Hughes and Menna Richards. In recent years I have been called upon to comment on medico-legal issues, e.g. euthanasia, the 'Pill', organ donation, post-mortem examinations and removal of organs, test-tube babies etc. etc. Media personnel, especially the researchers, work very hard and it is always a pleasure to be of assistance to them. Television is now in most homes and is ideal for the elderly – provided it doesn't cause them to sit for long periods. I remember visiting a patient in a farmhouse in rural Cardiganshire and noticed that the television had a lot of dust on it. I asked my patient, 'Do you watch television much?'

'No,' she said. 'I am going to buy a new one. I don't like the programmes on this one.'

I have done three runs of 'Doc-Slot' on radio. The first was many years ago on Radio Wales or maybe it was Radio Cymru. Much later Radio Ceredigion was established in Aberystwyth and on the very first day of this new service (14 December 1992), with Lyn Ebenezer asking the questions (set by me!), I had a six and a half-minute slot. This went on for 52 weeks and I was amazed how many local people tuned in to this feature. Later I did another three months extended 'Doc-Slot' with Trystan ab Ifan, another excellent interviewer, and this time I had 25 minutes airtime which was very nice. The trouble with comments within a news bulletin, which I do very often, is that the time allowed is only one-and-a-half to two minutes, if that! All good fun but stressful work, particularly when I have to deal with complex legal terms translated into Welsh.

The series of talks I gave on Radio Ceredigion were geared to what was topical at that particular time of the year. For example, my topic on 21 December 1992 was Christmas and I advised on drinking and eating to excess, and reminded the women to make sure that their Pill prescription did not run out over the holiday period. I also warned about driving after drinking alcohol, and gave advice on how to cope with the inevitable hangover. I ended with a reminder to keep all tablets out of sight and to beware of falling over toys which the grandchildren had been given over Christmas.

I dealt in turn with common conditions which worry or interest people, such as cancer, heart attacks, smoking, inability to sleep, gout, AIDS, organ donation, child abuse, old age, holidays overseas, anorexia, backache, infertility, hay fever, headaches, rheumatism, myalgic-encephalomyelitis (ME), accidents in the home, skin diseases, mental ill-health, etc. – 52 topics in all. This, in my opinion, was a valuable form of health education because health topics always command an audience. I suspect that it is true that the public learn far more about themselves and their illnesses from television and the radio than from their doctors.

Local radio is a wonderful opportunity for young people to 'cut their teeth' but the service in general must have a professional standard. Nowadays we have far too many TV channels. Viewing should be selective, especially for children. Television can be educational. As one middle-aged man once said: 'I find television very educational. When it is on I go to another room and read a book!'

A long time ago I was asked to take part in a television programme on a Sunday night in Cardiff. I arrived in the studio, which was an old chapel, about an hour before time and went along to the canteen alongside the studio. Two young ladies were sitting at a table drinking coffee. I asked them if they were taking part in the broadcast and one of them said, 'Yes, I have to sing and I am very nervous.' I told her that I was also nervous and joined them for some coffee. In the studio the first item on the programme was one of the young ladies from the canteen singing 'Amazing Grace'. She was none other than Iris Williams, now a world famous singer.

One of the other three members taking part in that particular programme was Mrs Dora Herbert Jones who interviewed me when I applied for an Army grant to enter medical college (See Chapter 5).

I benefited in an unexpected way from broadcasting. Many times 'on the air' I said that a drink of whisky at night was beneficial. I added that this was a nightly habit of mine. When I retired I received 58 bottles of whisky from my patients!

CHAPTER 10

'DRUNK-IN-CHARGE'

For many years, in addition to my GP work, I was the unofficial police surgeon. This meant being called to the Police Station when a 'medical' problem arose, e.g. mental instability or examination of a drunken man found in the gutter. In that case I had to certify whether or not the man was 'fit to be detained'. This was a difficult question because the heavily intoxicated man was often stuperose and too drunk to feel any pain. There were occasions when, after certifying that a man was fit to be detained, I would worry in case the police telephoned me some hours later to say that the man had died. Fortunately it did not happen to me, but a drunken man in the gutter could have had a stroke, a heart attack or an internal injury, the symptoms masked by alcoholic intoxication.

The commonest thing that I had to decide was whether a car driver, invariably male, was, 'under the influence of a drink or a drug to such an extent as to be incapable of having proper control of a car.'

Examination of the 'drunk-in-charge' was most unsatisfactory and the doctor carried a heavy responsibility. The doctor had to carry out a full medical examination because the common defence was that the man was ill, not drunk. Many of these cases elected to go for trial before a jury (Quarter Sessions in those days) and cross-examination was 'fierce' to say the least! The doctor was obliged to carry out certain tests to indicate alcoholic intoxication. These included manner of walking straight – irregular, over-precise, staggering, reeling or with feet wide apart; the reaction time to an order to turn; and the manner of turning – does the examinee keep his balance, lurch forward, or reel to one side? Their ability to stand with eyes open and eyes closed was also tested, as was their ability to pick up objects from the floor, etc. It is obvious that these tests, if positive, could also be caused by illness (sudden or chronic) and hence the importance of a full medical examination. There was nothing defending counsel would like better than demonstrating to the jury that the doctor had not examined the accused properly and the case could then be dismissed. Add to this the well-known reluctance of the 'Cardiganshire Jury' to convict because some of them could say 'there but for the Grace of God go I.' To add to my problems the examination of the drunk-in-charge was invariably at around midnight.

The examination above followed a pattern set out by the British Medical Association (BMA) in a booklet *Recognition of Intoxication*, first published in 1935 and revised in 1958. In this booklet the following paragraph appears:

It [the BMA] cannot conceive of any circumstances in which it could be considered safe for a person to drive a vehicle on the public roads with a level [of alcohol in the tissues] greater than 150mg/100ml.

The figure was translated as equivalent to 4½ pints of beer or 5 single whiskies. Note the upper level suggested in 1958 – 150mg% – compared with the legal limit in blood of 80mg% subsequently introduced. It was my usual practice to obtain a sample of urine, but the result would not be available for some days and I had to decide there and then whether the man was fit to drive. I well remember one case where the driver passed all the tests; he was allowed to go home in his car and was found dead 30 minutes later with his car halfway up a telegraph pole. I had long come to the conclusion that the tests we had to do were useless. To test this belief I arranged for four Corporation dustmen to drink measured amounts of beer – up to 4½ pints – between 6.00 and 9.00 pm and I examined them at 10.00 pm. They all passed the tests! At this time I was Secretary of the Aberystwyth Branch of the BMA and I asked our members for permission to propose the following motion at the Annual Meeting of the BMA held in Edinburgh (1959). This was the motion:

> That, having regard to the known effects on the motorist of alcohol intoxication and to the present unsatisfactory application of the law relating to the 'drunk-in-charge', it is recommended that a Royal Commission be appointed to investigate all aspects of this matter and in particular consider the introduction of a legal standard of blood alcohol above which it would be an offence to drive.

The motion was well received – to my surprise! – and was accepted as a reference to the Council of the BMA. The Council was already thinking along these lines but it was not until eight years later that the 1967 Road Safety Act made it an offence to drive:

> whilst having more than a prescribed level of alcohol in the blood, regardless of the effect which this may have on the driver.

Note the words 'prescribed level' which from 1967 to the time of writing this book has been set at 80 milligrammes of alcohol in 100 millilitres of blood. This is sometimes expressed as 80mg%. Note also the words 'regardless of the effect which this may have on the driver.' The offence now is not being drunk but simply having more than 80mg% of alcohol in the blood. This is reflected in the Road Traffic Act 1988:

> a person shall be taken to be unfit to drive if his ability to drive properly is for the time being impaired.

Present day police surgeons have an easy task – all they have to do is to take a sample of blood. The driver will be guilty when alcohol in his breath, blood or urine exceeds the prescribed limit. Using the term 'prescribed limit' enables Parliament to change the limit as and when required. It is highly probable that the 80mg% limit will be reduced to 50mg%. This has been the advice of the BMA and also the Association of Chief Police Officers to 'bring Britain into line with many other European Countries.' I like to believe that the Aberystwyth motion pushed things forward. My personal opinion, which very few people will agree with, is that people should not drive at all after drinking alcohol, even minimal amounts.

When the new law was enacted I gave up my police duties because the police doctor had to sign a contract to be available on demand and/or appoint a deputy. A few days after giving up my police duties the telephone rang at about 11.30 pm. My wife answered it. 'Police station here. Can I speak to the doctor please?' I heard this and whispered to my wife, 'Tell him I am out on a call.' She did. The Sergeant, who knew me well then said, 'Can I then speak to the man in bed with you?'

The Road Traffic Act controls driving not only under the influence of alcohol but also of drugs and many of these are doctor-prescribed medicinal drugs such as Valium, Librium, Oxazepam and a host of other benzodiazepines. To prove, in the police station, that a person is under the influence of drugs is very difficult, I would say well nigh impossible. Patients must be warned about the possible effects of these drugs even 24 hours after taking them, and told that the effects are enhanced by alcohol. This is a task for the prescribing doctor and for the pharmacist who dispenses the prescription. This warning appeared in the doctor's 'Bible', the indespensible *Monthly Index of Medical Specialities,* in July 2000:

> The [drugs as above] are widely used as hypnotics [sleeping tablets] because of their low incidence of adverse effects …
> However, the long acting compounds can induce residual sedative effects the next day and can accumulate, especially in the elderly.

I spent a lot of my time in court, Magistrates' courts, Quarter Sessions, and in the Coroner's court as a follow-up to the post-mortem examinations which I did for about twelve years. This experience proved invaluable when I embarked on a study of the law.

APPENDIX TO CHAPTER 10

This is the report *The Scotsman*, 21 July 1959, carried of my views put before the Annual Meeting of the British Medical Association in Edinburgh.

A motion by Dr J. H. Hughes, Aberystwyth, recommending that a Royal Commission be set up to investigate all aspects of the 'present unsatisfactory application of the law relating to the "drunk-in-charge"' was referred to the council.

The motion asked that the commission would especially consider the introduction of a legal standard of blood alcohol, above which it would be an offence to drive.

GROSSLY INEFFICIENT

Dr Hughes said that, in his opinion, the system practised in this country of determining whether the motorist was under the influence of drink was grossly inefficient and out of step with scientific advances. 'The procedure is not only unsatisfactory, but also grossly unfair,' he added. 'The fate of the motorist is entirely in the hands of the examining doctor, and the jury will not convict against the evidence of the doctor.'

The doctor, therefore, became judge and jury. If we are going to assist the course of justice, then we must be certain that we are doing it properly,' he said. 'The only system that I can visualise is a legal standard of blood alcohol above which it would be an offence to drive.'

He had no doubt that the time would come when the

legal standard would be adopted. 'Let us take the initiative,' he said, 'and bring this matter to the attention of the Government now, however much the result will cause us personal sacrifice.'

Dr R. E. Wright-St Clair, New Zealand, said that the motion was contrary to the spirit of British justice. 'We all know that the same blood level will have different effects on the driving ability of different persons and indeed on the same person in different cases,' he pointed out.

CHAPTER 11

THE STORY OF TUBERCULOSIS IN WALES

A whole book could be written on the history of tuberculosis in Wales, and the following account of how Wales tackled the problem 50 years before effective drugs became available is, of necessity, very brief.

Tuberculosis (TB) was referred to as the Captain of the Men of Death. In Welsh the word *Dicâd* (Decay) was used, as was, more frighteningly, *Darfodedigaeth*, the end. Consumption was another term used. The three worst affected counties in Wales were Merionethshire, Cardiganshire and Carmarthenshire. According to Dr Evan Evans of Tal-sarn's report in 1907, at the end of the 19th century and the early 20th century, these three counties, taken together, had about 700 deaths from TB every year. In the Borough of Aberystwyth only, 179 people died of tuberculosis in the period 1897-1906 (*Reports of the Borough Medical Officer of Health, Aberystwyth*). There was no curative treatment in the first half of the 20th century and it was thought that the disease was genetically determined. That is not so. It spreads by close family contact – hence the belief that it 'runs in the family'. It also spreads by close contact between people outside the home and, above all, among school children.

TB is of two types: pulmonary – from the lungs – spread by close contact, coughing and spitting, and bovine, spread by milk from cows affected by TB. This affects the bones, neck glands, kidneys, etc. In Cardiganshire, the majority of the people were very poor and lived in small, overcrowded houses with small windows. If the father had TB he would not be able to work and the family had to go *ar y plwyf* 'on the parish'. This was a small poor law paymen, the amount being determined by 'the gentry'. There was a reluctance to accept this payment, and it was not unusual for cases of TB to be 'hidden' because of the belief that the disease was a curse on the family. Even in my time some patients used to say, 'What have I done to deserve this?' when I had to tell them that they had a serious disease. This attitude probably had a Biblical origin.

The social conditions in rural Cardiganshire, and elswhere, were a major factor in the spread of the disease. The Medical Officer of Health (MOH) for Aberystwyth Borough wrote in his annual report for 1907:

> the incidence of tuberculosis is very high ... main causes ... lack of light and air, insufficient ventilation, overcrowding, insufficient dietary, probably an infected milk supply, poor working conditions [lead mines].

The MOH was presenting his report to the Borough Council. He said that the death rate from tuberculosis in the past year was 9.4. One of the Councillors got up. 'Mr Mayor,' he said, 'what does the doctor mean by 9.4 people dying? I can understand 9 people dying but not 0.4. Ask the doctor to explain.'

'Quite simple,' said the Mayor. 'There is no need to ask the doctor. I will explain. What he is saying is that out of 1,000 people in this Borough 9 died of tuberculosis and 4 were on the point of dying.'

In 1901 King Edward VII became Patron of a new organisation, the National Association for the Prevention of Tuberculosis. This organisation had a strong branch in the Carmarthenshire area. They built the first Sanatorium in Wales at Alltymynydd, near Llanybydder. It was completed in 1908 and had 20 beds. A Sanatorium was a special hospital where the patient could have complete rest of body and mind, ample feeding and 'pure air'.

In 1910 King Edward VII died. Mr David Davies, MP for Montgomeryshire and grandson of David Davies, Llandinam, who brought the railway towards Aberystwyth, was asked to call all the Lord Lieutenants of Wales together in order to arrange a memorial in memory of the late King. Mr Davies added to the Committee representatives of public bodies. At this meeting Mr Davies referred to the interest the late king had taken in tuberculosis and his concern at the very high death rate. He suggested that the most appropriate memorial to the King would be to build a Sanatorium in every county in Wales. The Committee accepted this. The people of Wales contributed £204,000 for this venture and ultimately 17 Sanatoria were built, and financial help given towards the appointment of a TB physician and a TB nurse in each county. There were also visiting stations in the outlying areas. A new organisation was set up to control the spread of tuberculosis, which was called The King Edward VII Welsh National Memorial Association. Later, with government and local authority help, two large Sanatoria were built – one in Llangwyfan (220 beds) and one in Talgarth (300 beds). Later still, Sully Hospital was built near Cardiff to teach medical students about TB, and this hospital became a centre of excellence for the surgical treatment of the disease. David Davies also financed a Chair of Tuberculosis in the Medical School in Cardiff, the first of its kind in the world.

The next step was to educate the population about TB and its prevention. Public lectures were arranged and talks given to children in the schools. The school children had slates to write on and they cleaned them by spitting on the slate and wiping it off with their sleeve. This was stopped, and also 'DO NOT SPIT' notices went up in buses and trains. Another major step forward was to set up the Mass Radiography Service, a mobile X-ray unit that travelled throughout Wales. People were invited to attend for a chest X-ray and they looked forward to receiving the result, 'O.K. Today'. Some had the reverse message and were called for medical examination. When this service was inaugurated, David Davies, then Lord Davies, was the first to be X-rayed and it was revealed that he had a serious disease. He died soon afterwards at the age of 64.

The isolation and good nursing care of the TB patient in a Sanatorium meant that the death rate was coming down before the discovery of an antibiotic called Streptomycin which completely changed the picture. This drug was first used in a clinical trial in 1947. The results were so dramatic that the trial was abandoned and the drug used for the treatment of the disease. The National Health Service came into being in 1948 and all medication was free when clinically necessary. Added to this was the Clean Milk Campaign that gave rise to Tuberculin Tested Milk and the slaughter of cows testing positive for TB. Suddenly TB ceased to be a problem, and the organisation that made this possible will have a place of honour in the history of Wales.

POSTSCRIPT

Tuberculosis is on the way back, mainly among the homeless – the same social conditions which led to the spread of the disease in Britain in the 19th and early 20th centuries. The combination of AIDS and tuberculosis is a major problem, especially in the Third World. The drugs used are becoming less effective because of drug resistant strains of the TB germ. There is increasing evidence that badgers are spreading bovine TB and this is being urgently investigated. If this proves to be the case, badgers must be culled. Farmers are naturally worried because since 1986, according to *The Daily Telegraph*, 10 January, 2001, nearly 30,000 cattle have been destroyed to try to curb TB.

CHAPTER 12

RETIREMENT

At 23.59 hrs on 31 December 1986 I retired from medical practice. I was then exactly 65 years old and had been a doctor in active practice for 32 years. I had prepared myself for retirement. My work with the police and the Coroner meant that I had to attend court very often – the Magistrate's court, Quarter Sessions, Coroner's court and, once only, the civil court. Anyone who has attended a court knows that he will waste a lot of time waiting for his case to come up. As a rule I was allowed into the court, rather than having to wait in the corridor outside, and I could listen to what was going on. I got very interested and, in the course of time, I considered the possibility of taking up a study of the law after retirement. The possibility became a certainty when, returning from a postgraduate course in London, I picked up a book from the station bookstall. It was called *Lord Denning: The Family Story*, a paperback edition dated 1982. The book was described as 'The fascinating life of one of the great judges of modern times.' I read the book and then I had no hesitation. I had to embark on a study of the law. I changed the spelling of the word 'Retire' to 'Re-tyre' – I put on new tyres so as to allow myself to go further!

I enrolled on a correspondence course with the National Extension College (Cambridge), on the subject of 'General Principles of English Law'. The day after I retired was New Year's Day, which I took off as a holiday. On 2 January 1987 I started systematic study of the correspondence course. I was allocated to a Law Tutor in Sheffield and he marked and commented on my course essays. He was strict but always encouraging, and I found the whole course not only interesting but also exactly what I wanted at that stage. I completed the course in July 1987 and, at about this time, I read about a new course about to start in the Cardiff Law School. It was called 'Legal Aspects of Medical Practice'. I applied and was told that there were over 300 applicants for the course and only 24 would be enrolled. It was a great joy to me that I was one of the 24. When I registered at the University I was given the same University number that I had been given when I enrolled as a medical student 40 years before in 1947.

On this course, which was confined to people who had a basic degree relating to health care, we had six doctors, four dentists, four nurses, four pharmacists, two lawyers, two health administrators and two medical journalists. I was the oldest in the class and we all worked very hard. One of the doctors died. Three years later all but two graduated with the degree of Master of Law. The subjects taught and analysed included Medical Negligence, Damages, No-Fault Compensation, Clinical Trials, Consent to Treatment, Euthanasia, Mental Health Law, Abortion Law, Forensic Medicine, AIDS, Employment Law, Confidentiality, Self Regulation of Doctors, the law relating to drugs, and the legal aspects of family planning, covering topics such as contraception, sterilisation and in vitro fertilisation (test tube babies). It was a very interesting course and very topical. In the field of litigation, we are following America where patients sue for the simplest deviation from normal. In the old days, if something went wrong, the family would say, 'You did your best, Doctor.' Today they say nothing and a letter soon comes from their solicitor. It is obvious that where there has been negligence it is only right that the victim should be awarded damages. Damages are not a fine; they are calculated to ensure that the patient is able to live a life as near as possible to that he would have had if not injured, or cared for in the best possible manner by relatives supported by nursing and lay staff.

It is well recognised that doctors can make mistakes and they can never guarantee success in any operation or treatment. The law states that the doctor must exercise a reasonable degree of care and skill. He will not be found negligent if what he did, or did not do, is in accordance with a practice accepted as normal by 'a body of medical opinion skilled in that particular art'. Proving negligence is an uphill task. The victim (plaintiff) has to prove 'fault' – namely that the doctor did something wrong, and that the damage sustained was caused by that fault and nothing else. This is one of the reasons why these cases take such a long time to come to court. By the time they do some of the medical witnesses have left the area and may even be thousands of miles away, and the medical notes are often incomplete. What I consider unsatisfactory is that many of these cases are settled out of court on the morning of the court appearance, which suggests that this could have happened months, if not years, before.

A far better system, which I support, is Alternative Dispute Resolution, which can be briefly described as follows. As an alternative to going to court the victim, or 'next best friend', would be asked to appear before three experts who would consider the case and decide on its merits. Damages would be awarded where appropriate. The three experts would be a top lawyer, a top doctor, and a top-ranking layman. The patient would have to choose at the outset between going to court and appearing before the 'three wise men' as above. This system would save a vast amount of time and the fees of lawyers but maybe there are too many lawyers in Parliament for this to come about! The patient should have a choice because for many patients a quick settlement would be better than a long wait for a court case with its uncertain outcome.

A House of Commons public accounts committee highlighted the extent of the problem associated with medical negligence in a report in the *BMJ* in 2000. This stated that in 1997-8 £79m had been paid out in negligence cases in England with outstanding liabilities estimated at £2.8bn. In Wales the position is correspondingly worse. In the year 1997-8 it was estimated that the litigation bill would be £145m, which would be a drastic increase from £78m in the previous year (*Western Mail* 1999). A Welsh Risk Pool operates in Wales where Health Authorities and NHS

Trust hospitals pay a premium into a 'pool' which will help them meet the cost of medical negligence claims. During 1999-2000 the collective sum paid by these authorities was £13m. Without such a risk pool it would be impossible for an NHS Trust to finance some of the awards given against it. For example, in 1998, a boy aged 11 was awarded £3.28m after suffering complications at birth which left him with cerebral palsy (*Western Mail* 2000). The trend towards suing doctors has obviously contributed to a debt in the NHS in Wales – £74m in the financial year 1999-2000 – and this is money lost to medical care. The latest figures show that the NHS paid out £400m in claim settlements in 1999 (*Daily Telegraph* 2001). The fear of litigation leads doctors to practise defensive medicine, which is unnecessary, wastes money and could harm the patient. Court cases involving medical negligence are headline news but it is noteworthy that 90% are settled out of court, as the damaged patients receive compensation at the time when they need it most.

To return to my study of the law. When I was a student in Cardiff I did some of my work in the law library in Aberystwyth. Mr John Williams, now Professor and Head of Department, had an interest in medical law. He was at that time a Senior Lecturer in Family Law and was a brilliant lecturer. He set out a proposed syllabus for teaching medical law to undergraduates in Aberystwyth which was approved. In 1991 I was appointed an Honorary Lecturer in Medical Law and it was most interesting to take part in the lectures and seminars. We had huge classes, about 140 students, and the seminars had to be repeated six times. Since 1999 my main role has been to act as a link between medicine and the law and it is a great pleasure and honour to serve Prof John Williams in this way.

When I finished the course in Cardiff the old question presented itself again: What next? Some of the law lecturers in Aberystwyth suggested (insisted) that I undertook a research project for a PhD degree. I did. It took about five years and I graduated yet again. This was my fourth degree from the University of

Wales and I can now say – no more examinations! I was most fortunate that my wife, Elinor, helped me with proof reading my last dissertation, which ran to about 100,000 words. It was a most interesting part of my life and I am indebted to the Law Departments in Cardiff and Aberystwyth for encouragement and support. My task now is to keep up-to-date in medical law because I am called upon by the media to comment on contemporary problems – of which there are many! By 'media' I mean local radio, BBC Wales, Welsh and English radio, Radio Cymru, S4C and ITV. In the tax year 1999-2000, I did over 50 of these interviews.

I will now discuss as briefly as possible two medico-legal topics which are very much in the news and are to a certain extent controversial.

1 EUTHANASIA

The word actually means an 'easy death' but the general public look upon it as 'mercy killing'. It is certainly not mercy killing because killing anyone is unlawful. If the intent is to kill, the charge is murder. If the person is found guilty, the punishment is a mandatory sentence of life imprisonment. The problem that exists in medical practice is the management of the terminally ill patient who is in pain and needs increasing doses of powerful drugs, which will control the pain but will bring on death earlier than would otherwise be the case. The intent here is to relieve pain, death is not the aim, and this is looked upon as good medical practice. The word 'intent' is a razor's edge between good medical practice and a charge of murder. The doctor's duty is to do his best for the patient and that sometimes means an earlier death as a consequence of pain-relieving medication. The Golden Rule is that good medical care aims to end patients' suffering not their lives.

In a leading case in the UK a rheumatologist, Dr Cox, had a 70 year old patient with very severe rheumatoid arthritis. She was being given a large dose of diamorphine – up to 50 mg every hour – but she was still in constant pain. She 'howled and screamed like a dog' when touched. She told the doctor that she could not go on any longer and asked him to give her something to die. Her two sons were at her bedside and they supported their mother in her request. The doctor gave her a very large dose of diamorphine but it had no effect. He then gave her an injection containing Potassium Chloride, which has no pain-killing effect, and which he must have known could only cause death. This took place within two minutes. A nurse on the ward reported the doctor to the hospital management but delayed doing so for three days. In the meantime, the body was cremated. This meant that the doctor was not charged with murder but with the lesser charge of attempted murder. A jury found the doctor guilty. When cases like this come to court judges are generally very considerate and sympathetic – they tend to hold fast to common sense. In this particular case the doctor was sentenced to prison for 12 months (suspended). The Judge said, 'What you did was not only criminal, it was a total betrayal of your duty as a physician.' (R v Cox 1992)

The suspended sentence meant that the criminal court had 'tempered justice with mercy', and this was the attitude of the General Medical Council when Dr Cox appeared before his 'ethical' court. Dr Cox was later allowed to return to work on condition that he undertook further training in pain relief therapy, and that he worked under a 'mentor' for 12 months. His employing authority imposed these conditions.

The other important case was that of Tony Bland, aged 22, who had been in a coma since being crushed in the Hillsborough Football Stadium three years previously. He was in a 'persistent vegative state', which meant that his brain was destroyed but he could breathe on his own; he had difficulty in swallowing, could not see, or hear, or feel pain. He was fed through a tube and he had no hope of recovery. The doctors in charge and the parents, who visited every day, wanted to stop the feeding tube and let Tony die. The doctors applied to the High Court for a ruling on the legality of withdrawing tube feeding. The Judge ruled that the artificial nutrition together with any other treatment could be withdrawn except: '. . . for the purpose of enabling Mr Bland to end his life and to die peacefully with the greatest dignity and the least distress.' (Airedale NHS Trust v Bland 1993).

The case went to the Appeal Court and, because of its importance, to the House of Lords. The question arose why death by commission is murder but death by omission could be good medical practice. There is a difference, as Lord Goff in the House of Lords judgment said:

> The doctor who is caring for such a patient [Mr Bland] ... cannot be under an absolute obligation to prolong his life by any means available to him, regardless of the quality of the patient's life. Common humanity requires otherwise ... the doctor, in discontinuing life support, is simply allowing his patient to die of his pre-existing condition. (Airdale NHS Trust v Bland 1993).

In other words, removing the feeding tube allowed Tony Bland to die from the injuries he had received three years previously. This is the law and it comes back to the basic principle that in the case of an unconscious adult, the doctor will not be acting unlawfully if he acts in his patient's best interests and, by inference, best interests can sometimes mean being allowed to die.

There is a system of voluntary euthanasia available in Holland which I support. Doctors may comply with a patient's wish to die provided that the patient is seriously ill and expected to die within 6 months. The patient must *repeatedly* ask to die and the family must be informed. The patient's terminal condition needs to be confirmed by a doctor from outside the practice and, when the patient has died under these conditions, the case has to be referred to the Coroner to check that the official guidelines (now the law) have been complied with. This arrangement appears to me to be simple, sensible, and an example of a doctor acting in his patient's best interests.

To die or not to die, that is the question, to paraphrase Shakespeare. It is not really a question because we must realise that death is a natural phenomenon. We tend to be afraid of death, or to be more precise, we are afraid of the process of dying. The American film actor and director, Woody Allen, expressed something we all hope for when he said, 'It's not that I'm afraid to die. I just don't want to be there when it happens.'

Good medical practice can ensure that the patient is not 'there when it happens.' How? Simply stated, it involves the principle of 'double effect': a doctor cannot kill a patient to relieve pain, but he can give increasing amounts of pain killing drugs to alleviate pain and mental discomfort in terminal cases, even if he knows that the drugs given will hasten death.

There is increasing interest in the 'Living Will'. I prefer to call it an 'Advance Declaration'. This enables anyone over 18 to declare, when they are clear in their mind, how they would like to be treated when dying and unable to speak for themselves. Under Common Law the Living Will is legally binding only if the declaration made fits exactly the condition the patient is in at the material time. This is what the prospective patient, that means anyone of us, declares when he signs a 'Living Will':

> If the time comes when I can no longer take part in decisions for my own future, let this declaration stand as the testament to my wishes.

> If there is no reasonable prospect of my recovery from physical illness or impairment expected to cause me severe distress or to render me incapable of rational existence, I request that I be allowed to die and not be kept alive by artificial means and that I receive whatever quantity of drugs which may be required to keep me free from pain or distress even if the moment of death is hastened.

In the last resort it is important that the patient has confidence and faith in the doctor. This story is an example of faith going a bit too far. A patient had been ill for a long time. One evening his wife telephoned the doctor saying that her husband was now very ill.

'I will come at once,' said the doctor.

The doctor went to the bedroom. He stood on the right side

of the bed, the man's wife on the other side. The patient was lying on his back in bed, eyes closed, deathly pale, mouth wide open, top teeth fallen down. The doctor felt for a pulse and after a while turned to the wife and said, 'I'm afraid your husband is dead.'

The old boy opened his eyes and said, 'No, doctor, I was only having a little nap.'

His wife bent down to her husband and said, 'Shut up, Tom. Do you think you know better than the doctor!'

2 CONSENT

A patient's consent to treatment was totally ignored in my early days as a doctor. It was a case of 'Doctor Knows Best' or medical paternalism as it is known today. Even the Hippocratic oath suggests that compliance was the norm: 'I will prescribe regimen for the good of my patients according to my ability and my judgment.'

Note the words 'my judgment'. It is only in fairly recent years that obtaining informed consent to any operation or medical procedure has become part of the doctor's duty of care to his patient. Consent must be 'informed' because you can't consent to something unless you know what you are consenting to, and the patient has a right according to *A Charter for Patients in Wales* published by the Welsh Office in 1991, 'to be given a clear explanation of any treatment proposed, including any risks and any alternatives, before you decide whether you will agree to the treatment.'

The basic principle of law involved is that our bodies belong to us and no-one, except in an emergency, can 'touch' us without permission. Patients sign a consent form when in hospital. Do they understand what they read? Very rarely. They may not have their glasses on when they sign, and patients are afraid to ask questions. The signature on the consent form is useless unless the 'mind goes with the signature'. (Thurston G. 'The Problems of Consent.' *BMJ* 1966). Consent forms have recently been re-worded and the 'catch all' clause which stated that the patient consents 'to such further or alternative measures as may be found to be necessary' has been omitted. The new form gives the patient control of what should *not be done* without prior consultation.

We have seen in the UK in the last few years an explosion of cases involving lack of consent to a surgical or medical procedure. For example, taking out a uterus because of a suspicion of a tumour associated with it, sterilisation at the time of a Caesarean operation or the removing of a normal appendix at the time of a hysterectomy just in case it gives trouble later. The same applies to giving a child the MMR vaccine because there is no measles vaccine for use on its own and the mother being aware of possible ill effects of this combined vaccine (Crohn's Disease and Autism – suspected but not proved). The mother or guardian, has a legal right to refuse the injection for her child and she must not be coerced in any way.

To complicate matters the doctor has a legal right, known as therapeutic privilege, to withhold from a patient information that is likely to upset the patient and increase the anxiety and concern about the medical condition that needs attention. This is a privilege and the doctor should not hide behind it. I will illustrate this dilemma with a typical example of the difficulties sometimes associated with informed consent and whether this translates to valid consent: Clinical Trials, 'Human Guinea Pigs' in common parlance. Why do we need to experiment? The major advances in medicine during the second half of the 20th century came about as a result of medical need and scientific curiosity. The doctor as a scientist has an inquisitive mind and, of necessity, this means an element of experimentation. This starts by recognising a problem. A hypothesis is constructed. This is tested in the laboratory, then on animals, on healthy volunteers, and finally on the patients who have the disease for whom the new treatment is designed. Medical experimentation is essential for the good of mankind, but the outcome of an experiment can never be guaranteed. The object of a clinical trial is to find out whether the drug is safe and whether it is effective as a treatment. A trial is an adventure into the unknown and it is inevitable that some people will be damaged by side effects and some will die.

Now for the problem. Should patients be told that they are taking part in a trial? The vast majority of people would say 'Yes' but when the mechanics of the trial is explained to them very many will refuse to take part. Take cancer of the breast. Simply but bluntly stated, we still don't know what is the best treatment for this disease. Clinical trials are on-going in this country and overseas. In the majority of cases of cancer of the breast it is not necessary to remove the whole breast, but merely to remove the 'lump' plus or minus the glands in the axilla (armpit).

Should the surgery above be followed by additional treatment to deal with any cancerous cells which may have spread elsewhere in the body? Trials in the past have tested the advantages of chemotherapy, or radiotherapy, or a combination of both, or no additional treatment. Patients are allocated to the alternative treatments by 'blind' computer allocation. This is what patients usually object to, especially when the computer allocates them to 'no treatment'. The patient allocated to 'no treatment' does not realise that she may be better off at the end of five years than patients allocated to the other treatments. That was certainly true in the early trials involving chemotherapy and radiotherapy.

There is a measure of control over clinical trials in that a Local Ethics Committee must approve the trial. Members of the Committee do not see the patient and cannot really know whether the consent for the trial is a valid consent. Animals are far better off than human beings when it comes to experimentation. There is statutory control; the Animals (Scientific Procedures) Act 1986, ensures that every research project is approved by the Home Office and that inspectors call to check on the welfare of the animals concerned. At the end of every year a full report is submitted to the Home Office and this is laid before Parliament. We need a similar system of control for human 'guinea-pigs'. There is at the moment very little effective control and even less accountability.

Consent is of increasing importance today because the Health Authorities insist that all medication must be 'evidence based', and the only way to ascertain this, and possible side effects, is by clinical trials. Patients must realise that every treatment is a carefully controlled balance of risks, a point made very succinctly in an editorial in *World Medicine* 27 January 1979:

> If a drug has no side effects it is unlikely to have much therapeutic effects either. No train journey is absolutely safe; no surgical procedure is entirely free from risks. Yet the public and politicians demand absolute safety from the pharmaceutical industry and so prevent therapeutic advances.

That was written in 1979. It is more or less the position today. How does the doctor solve the dilemma? The Bible suggests the answer: 'Treat others as you want them to treat you.' Matthew: 7.12.

CHAPTER 13

HUMAN FERTILISATION – LEGAL AND ETHICAL ASPECTS

On 25 July 1978 Louise Brown was born. She was the first 'test-tube' baby and on that day science fiction became reality. It was a major advance in medical science but the medical profession shunned the gynaecologist involved, Patrick Steptoe. Ten years later he was awarded the Gold Medal of the British Medical Association and a CBE in the Honours List but he died of cancer before he could receive either of the awards.

I clearly remember the day Louise was born. Television, radio and the newspapers carried the story. In my morning surgery on that day I asked the ten consecutive men that came to consult me what they thought of the test tube baby. They all had the same answer: they preferred the old fashioned method! As expected there was a hue and cry in the country. The cry was 'This is unethical!' 'It is not natural!' 'It must be banned!'

When there is a major problem of this nature the government sets up a Committee to look into it. In this case it was the Warnock Committee, who was asked to suggest possible legislation. The Warnock Committee reported very quickly but legislation was not enacted until the Human Fertilisation and Embryology Act 1990 (HFE Act) which now controls all aspects of in vitro fertilisation (IVF). The HFE Act created a statutory body which deals with registration and control of centres where IVF takes place and deals with the many legal and ethical problems that inevitably arise from a major scientific breakthrough such as this. When embryos are formed artificially in a petri dish (not a test tube) there will usually be more than are required for implantation. What should be done with any spare embryos?

Why are there spare embryos? The women involved have to have injections to stimulate the ovaries to produce eggs (ova). It is not unusual for five or six ova to be harvested. All these ova can be fertilised in the petri dish but not all of them can be implanted. It is pointless implanting one embryo in the womb – it will not 'take' – so two embryos (sometimes three) are introduced and that is why one in three cases of test-tube babies results in a multiple birth.

So what do we do with the spare embryos? The general public feared that they would be used for uncontrolled research. The Warnock Committee suggested, and this was accepted, that the embryos could be used for research up to 14 days old, and then destroyed. The spare embryos could be stored for future implantation, donated to another woman, or thrown away. There was also concern in the country that IVF could lead to 'designer' babies and this, together with sex selection, was banned. Cloning was also declared unlawful. All this is strictly controlled. Clinics and hospitals where IVF is performed are licensed and are visited at regular intervals by members of the statutory authority set up under the HFE Act. IVF is expensive and the overall success rate is very low, about 18% in the year 2000. Very few NHS hospitals undertake IVF because of the cost. Spare embryos can be stored in liquid nitrogen at minus 200°C and can be kept for years. It is not uncommon for a woman who has IVF to keep spare embryos and use these to have a second baby two years later. I have seen such a second child, who was perfectly normal and none the worse for having been in the deep freeze for two years!

One of the ethical problems that arises today is that some post-menopausal women want babies by this method. They have reached the stage in their lives when the house has been paid for, the BMW is in the drive, and there is ample money in the bank. There is no statutory upper limit but most clinics will not treat women over 55, which is the upper age limit suggested by the

HFE Authority. Should post-menopausal women receive this treatment? Should unmarried women have a baby in this way? The Fertilisation Act (HFE) requires that the welfare of any child born by IVF, including the need of a child for a father, must be taken into account. Feminists don't like this! The legal standard now is that the welfare of the child shall be paramount (*The Children Act 1989*).

Another ethical problem presented itself recently when a homosexual male couple were able to have a baby using a surrogate mother. The couple involved were English but the surrogate mother was in America. Surrogacy is where a woman carries a baby for someone else who cannot bear their own child – the 'rent-a-womb' method. The commissioning parents cannot pay the surrogate mother but can pay reasonable expenses. Such a surrogate arrangement is not a contract and cannot be enforced by the courts. When the child is born, irrespective of any financial payments or promises, the surrogate is the mother and this has caused problems when the surrogate is unwilling to surrender the child. The surrogate remains the mother of the child until the commissioning parents have adopted it in accordance with the law. There is a 'fast-track' adoption procedure in these cases.

There is a happy story of a woman who had been born without a womb but was otherwise fit and able to produce ova. Her husband was fertile. Her mother agreed to be the surrogate, and she gave birth to twins. She gave birth to her own grandchildren!

There is a 'sort of surrogacy' arrangement described in the Bible. The text is in Genesis and I will relate the story slightly modified by a Hughes translation from the ancient Greek! – with apologies to the original author.

When Rachel realised that she bore Jacob no children she envied her sister and said to Jacob, 'Give me children, or else I die.'

Jacob was annoyed by this request and he said to Rachel, 'Do you think I am God? It was He that decided you should be barren.'

Rachel then said, 'We have a maid, Bilhah. Why don't you go to bed with her and she can give me the baby?'

Jacob couldn't believe his luck. He ran upstairs to Bilhah's bedroom. And it came to pass that Bilhah had a son and he was given to Rachel. Rachel said, 'God heard my prayer and gave me a son. All praise to God.'

Jacob continued to visit the maid and another son was born and given to Rachel. Some months later Rachel was in the local supermarket pushing her first baby in the pushchair. She met the lady next door, Leah. Leah said, 'Oh, you have a baby.'

'Yes,' said Rachel, and she told Leah how this came about.

'Well,' said Leah. 'I am barren too. Do you think your Jacob would go to bed with my maid?'

'I can only ask,' said Rachel.

When Jacob was approached he again couldn't believe his luck. He had noticed that there was a very nice *au pair* girl next door. He jumped over the garden fence. And Leah's maid bore Jacob a son.

In the course of time Leah's maid bore Jacob a second son and both children were given to Leah because she was barren. Rachel and Leah were very happy (Genesis 30. 1-14).

All this did not do Jacob any harm. He was 147 years old when he died!

CHAPTER 14

DOCTOR IN THE COMMUNITY

A family doctor in a rural or small urban area, such as Aberystwyth, is very much part of the community. His children go to primary and secondary schools with other children and parents get to know each other through the Parent-Teacher Associations (PTA). When a child is born into the practice the doctor will have seen the mother for six to seven months during her pregnancy. He will also see her, after the baby's birth, in her own home. Later the baby is brought to the surgery for immunisation against the infectious diseases and, later still, mothers bring their children to the surgery with the usual plethora of childhood ailments, e.g. 'Won't eat', 'wets the bed', earache, coughs and various rashes. In this way the doctor gets to know the family, which is the true basis of medical practice.

Education is the bedrock of society and it is an absolute tragedy, and inexcusable, that even today, at the beginning of the 21st century, some children come out of school unable to read or write. We have been very fortunate in Aberystwyth in that we have had excellent education for the children, both at primary and secondary school level, and this applies to both English medium and Welsh medium schools.

An Anglican school was built in Aberystwyth in 1812 and replaced in 1866 with a new school, the National School. To cater for the non-Anglican children a Board school was opened in 1874, known as the Alexandra Road School (*A Fashionable Watering Place*, W.J. Lewis). There was a lot of rivalry between the Church schools in the country generally and the nonconformist schools, which were called Board schools, later Council schools. In Aberystwyth a similar rivalry extended to the linguistic sphere and Alexandra Road School was divided into a Welsh primary and an English primary school. An 'iron curtain' divided the two sections. The PTA did not like this arrangement and we, the English medium school parents, campaigned for a new school. The Education Committee said that we could have a new school if we found a site. After much hunting and consulting we settled for a site where the Rugby Club is now. Three of us parents went as a deputation to the Town Hall to put our case, the three of us being Henry Read, John Phillips and myself. Alderman Richard Ellis was in the chair. We told him about the proposed site for the school. He said, 'You can't have that site, it is liable to flooding. I will give you a better site.' That is what happened. The site was ideal. In the course of time the school was built and opened in 1969. The parents decided that the new school should have a swimming pool and the PTA raised enough money to build a pool, which is still in use and supplements the municipal pool cum leisure centre which is adjacent to the school. Plas Crug school had, and continues to have, excellent, in fact outstanding, teachers. I must pay tribute especially to the work of the school's first Headmaster, Mr Ceiriog Evans, and to Mrs Rhiannon Steeds, an inspirational teacher, who later became Head of the school.

The excellent schools in Aberystwyth, and elsewhere in the County, were due in no small measure to the Director of Education, Dr J. Henry Jones. He was a classical scholar and made it his mission that all the children in the County should have the best possible education, despite debates in the Education Committee where some councillors were concerned about depopulation. It is on record that Alderman Gwarnant Williams said, 'If you want to keep the children in Cardiganshire, don't give them any education.' (*Welsh Gazette*, 3 June, 1937)

Very true of course, but Dr Henry Jones would have no part in that. We owe a great debt to a far sighted Director of Education, and what he practised then was still a high priority when, in 1999, the Prime Minister, Mr Blair, said that high on the list in his Government's manifesto would be, 'Education. Education. Education.'

As already stated, the new school was opened in 1969 and as parents, we were very happy. A major problem surfaced in October 1968. The Local Education Authority (LEA) decided to change its education policy and, out of the blue, our children were given a leaflet, *Declaration of Policy on Language*, to take home to their parents. The contents of that leaflet, described as a 'bombshell if ever there was one' (Edgar Jones, *Cambrian News* 3 January, 1969), stated that there would be a change in Welsh teaching policy. Welsh was taught as a subject when the children came to school, which was generally acceptable, but the new policy declared:

> By the junior stage the children should have gained sufficient mastery over the second language to receive a part of their education through the medium of that language.

To teach other subjects through the medium of Welsh in an English-orientated school caused so many parents alarm and concern that an informal group was formed, which became the Cardiganshire Education Campaign with an initial membership of about 400, later 600, most, but not all, from the Aberystwyth area.

The Director of Education, Dr Henry Jones, addressed 'well attended' meetings in the local schools and he frankly admitted that 'the Declaration was ambiguous and awkwardly phrased,' (*Cambrian News* 24 January, 1969). He said that the LEA would re-word the Declaration. The amended version said:

> During the junior stage children will gain increasing competence in the second language through its use in the life and work of the school.

The amended Declaration did not materially change the situation and did not lend itself to strict interpretation. The parents were still very worried and the LEA made no official efforts to clarify its meaning. The parents looked upon this as compulsory teaching of Welsh as a subject (generally accepted) with a view to the child later being taught other subjects through the medium of Welsh. There was almost universal objection to this, especially in an English-orientated school.

There was another important factor. In Plas Crug school, around a third of the 300 odd pupils were incomers to the town, children of Civil Servants and postgraduate students from overseas attending the university for relatively short periods of time. There was a very large range of languages involved and the majority of the children had to be taught English before they could be taught in normal school classes. Parental concern increased and at St. Padarn's R.C. School in Aberystwyth a questionnaire answered by 152 out of 160 parents with children at the school showed that 94% did not want their children to be taught through the medium of Welsh (*Cambrian News* 24 January, 1969).

The Campaign appealed to the LEA and, later, to the Welsh Office, quoting *The Gittings Report on Primary Education in Wales*, August 1967, and referring to the Secretary of State's Circular which followed the Gittings Report. This Circular seemed to favour our viewpoint and two relevant paragraphs are quoted here:

Paragraph 4: the Secretary of State . . . thinks it would be valuable if all authorities were now to undertake an early review of their policies on the lines proposed in the Report … He hopes that in making these reviews authorities will undertake an objective evaluation of their linguistic needs in their area, neighbourhood by neighbourhood, taking into account the wishes of the parents in each neighbourhood.

Paragraph 6: The attention of authorities is also drawn to what is said in Recommendation 4 about opting out for parents who do not wish their child to be taught Welsh, and about the need to make clear to parents that they have this choice.

The Circular recommended action as above but it did not change the situation in Aberystwyth. The dispute overflowed into the local press and into one national newspaper, *The People*, in early February, which reported that one seven year old boy in another local school, Penparcau, 'has to ask the teacher in a language he does not understand – Welsh' when he wanted to go to the toilet. One of the teachers admitted to this totally unreasonable and extremist action. She was reported as saying, 'It's true. I encourage them to ask in Welsh . . . I persuade them to use the Welsh phrase before they go.' By the time the child is able to say, 'Gaf i fynd i'r toilet, os gwelwch yn dda?' it could well be too late!

There were no winners in this dispute but wise management by the teachers led to a balanced curriculum which became acceptable to the majority of parents.

So much for the school issue. What else did I do in, and for the community? Very early in my time in Aberystwyth I was invited to join the local Rotary Club. This is an international organisation and its aim is to become aware of the problems in the local community, nationwide, and overseas, and to do something about it. Pure water is essential for life and difficult to get in many countries overseas, as I know to my cost (see Chapter 5). Rotary has a long history of financing projects which aim to provide wells in villages, with a three-foot surrounding wall, a pump, and a cover to prevent contamination. Another on-going international project aims to rid the Third World of poliomyelitis and other childhood infectious diseases. This is the Polio-Plus campaign which has so far been very successful. Having spent some time in the African bush, I sometimes wonder whether the Polio-Plus campaign will keep the children alive merely to die of malnutrition later on. Provision of clean water, a mass contraception campaign and widespread education about AIDS would be more effective. That is my opinion, and mine alone!

I have also been involved in other organisations in the town, for example: Cancer Relief (MacMillan Nurses), Arthritis and Rheumatism Council, and Action Group for Mental Health – all worthwhile organisations. I am a very frequent speaker at clubs and meetings in this town and surrounding villages. I look upon these talks as a valuable source of health education. Members of the audience are mainly elderly people who want to keep healthy in order to avoid the dreaded residential or nursing home. The expectation of life is increasing rapidly. In the year 2000 it was 74 for men and 79 for women. Blessed are they that have a double-X chromosome! Anyone living beyond the ages quoted is, like me, living in 'injury time'!

Finally in this chapter there is the question of poverty. In Chapter 11, when discussing tuberculosis, I referred to the extreme poverty at the beginning of the 20th century. Poverty prevails and the family doctor is more aware of this than any other person. Why should people be poor today in a prosperous town like Aberystwyth? In my practice I became aware that poverty was the result of:

over commitment to hire purchase
excessive smoking and drinking alcohol
no reserve of money for the sudden emergency
single mothers with poor parental support – unusual
inability to cook wholesome meals with a lack of ability
to spend money wisely
long-term unemployment
people with an income just above the threshold for
income support

These are some of the problems that are presented, directly or indirectly, to the doctor, often by a woman requesting sleeping tablets. If asked why she can't sleep she ultimately blames relative poverty. Things are no better on a national scale. In an article in the *British Medical Journal* the Editor wrote, 'Britain has more children living in poverty than any other country in the European Union.' (*BMJ* 1999)

It is the children that are most at risk when the family income is below an acceptable level, and such a family is pushed further into poverty by the birth of another child. A state of poverty is defined as an income less than half the national average. Poverty has an adverse effect on health – the life expectancy is less, there is more illness in the family and, consequently, more days lost from school which may then lead to educational failure. These children, more often than not, have children when in their teens. The writer of the article quoted above ends by saying, 'Can Britain really abolish child poverty? The poor, says the Bible, will always be with us. But it would be hard to think of a better aim to unite people in Britain . . .'

The doctor in practice can enquire and give advice; he can involve the service organisations, Rotary, Round Table and the Lions Club etc., because these organisations include representatives of the professions and local businesses in their membership.

One answer to the problem is education. There is very little hope for young people who leave school with no qualifications and no hope in life. Helen Palmer, the brilliant archivist for Ceredigion in her article, 'Documentary Evidence on the Lives of the Poor', *Ceredigion* Vol XIII 1998, wrote:

> In studies of the Welsh language the significance of the fact that 'ladder' and 'school' are the same word 'ysgol' is often cited to illustrate the importance placed on education as a means of raising oneself socially.

One very simple way to help is to ensure that young people are taught how to cook nutritious meals and, equally important, to know how to spend money wisely. Too often the young people put their money 'into a purse with a hole in it'. (Haggai 1: 5-6) There is too much emphasis in the UK on university education at the expense of technical education. We need carpenters, electricians, plumbers, etc., but a successful apprenticeship depends on a basic educational standard. Work is always beneficial. Thomas Carlyle (1795-1881) had the correct message when he wrote, 'Blessed is he who has found his work; let him ask no other blessedness.'

CHAPTER 15

RANDOM THOUGHTS

I am conscious of the fact that I have left a lot of contemporary problems out of this book, and I will try to make amends by saying a little about some of the things that occupy my mind now.

NATIONAL HEALTH SERVICE

This is in crisis. We had no trouble at all when I was in practice but now there seems to be absolute chaos. The 'Trust' administration with its supplier/purchaser policy is not working and, in my opinion, it is not compatible with the service patients deserve, namely, quick access to medical expertise at all levels and beds being available within a reasonable time. This cannot be achieved if hospital beds are reduced to such an extent that non-urgent operations have to be cancelled whenever there is an emergency, e.g. a 'flu epidemic or a major road accident. A major mistake was to operate the 'Project 2000' system of training nurses, where nurses are trained in the classroom rather than working on the wards, the apprenticeship system. We need to bring back the Matron to our hospitals. The Matron and our excellent Ward sisters, trained as they were through the ranks, would render the service patients really need and expect.

We are relatively healthy as a nation today. This is not altogether due to doctors and nurses but rather to a better environment – good affordable houses, clean water, safe milk, pure and nutritious food, no overcrowding, an efficient sewer, good refuse collection system, clean air, contraception leading to smaller families, full employment whenever possible, and thus more money to buy food. This is called public health which was, to a certain extent, downgraded when the NHS was introduced in 1948.

The question is often asked, 'Can the NHS survive?' The answer must be, 'Yes.' The service will have to be reformed and it is possible that certain operations, e.g. transsexual surgery, cosmetic surgery, varicose veins and in vitro fertilisation will not be available free under the NHS. One thing is certain, the NHS is the best in the world and the service should continue to be free at the point of delivery. Rationing is inevitable and has always been with us. It must be accepted and it must be explicit. We should be proud of the NHS and thankful that a Welshman, Aneurin Bevan, was the politician who brought it into being.

POLYPHARMACY

This means taking a multitude of tablets at any one time. It is far too common today and can cause problems. Patients should not depend on repeat prescriptions unless the doctor is reviewing the medication at regular intervals. Many drugs have been withdrawn because of side effects which did not appear in clinical trials but became apparent much later. The motto should be, for doctors and patients, 'Remember Thalidomide.'

There are two examples of unconscious humour in relation to on-going medication:

Patient: 'Do I have to take these tablets as long as I live?'

Doctor: 'You certainly won't need them afterwards.'

I sent a lady to see a consultant regarding her heart. When she returned to my surgery I asked her, 'How did you get on?'

'He was a very nice doctor, but he frightened me,' she replied.

'Why do you say that?' I asked.

'Well,' she said, 'he gave me a prescription for tablets and said that I would have to take one every day for the rest of my life.'

'What's wrong with that?' I asked.

'He only gave me thirty!' she replied.

There is a regular tendency for patients to ask for new medication that has been talked about on television. My advice has always been, 'Don't rush to try new things. Let others be guinea pigs.' It is not always easy to say this, especially if the patient has some distressing and painful condition such as arthritis, multiple sclerosis, or psoriasis. Confucius (551-478 BC) had the right answer when he said:

> Because the newer methods of treatment are good, it does not follow that the old ones were bad; for if our honourable and wonderful ancestors had not recovered from their ailments, you and I would not be here today.

XENO-TRANSPLANTATION

A long word which means transplanting animal organs into human beings. There is a chronic shortage of human organs which can be used, and the pig is the best animal because the size of its organs, e.g. kidneys and heart, are almost the same size as in human beings. The pig heart valve has been used for replacement in humans for at least 25 years, and three of my patients had pig valves inserted and have been in good health ever since. There are two major problems to overcome before pig organs can be used more widely:

1 Pigs carry a virus which is harmless to the pig but the effect on human cells is unknown. It is a retrovirus, not unlike the AIDS virus, and more research is necessary. Every new venture has a cost/benefit equation but some people on renal dialysis would be prepared to take the risks because of the possible benefits. However, the pig virus could spread into the human population with disastrous results. This problem requires ethical consideration at a high level and is an example of the problems that doctors face when introducing new drugs or surgical procedures.

2 Another problem is the rejection of the pig organ by the human body. Pigs are being bred at the moment under controlled conditions and, by genetic modification, it is hoped that 'descendant' pigs will develop organs that can be trans-

planted without rejection. If this experiment is a success it will help solve the problem of organ donation because pigs breed quickly and can have large litters. The ability to clone the pig will be an added advantage. I see no ethical objections to this work; after all we eat pork and use insulin derived from the pancreas of the pig. To use pigs in this way may have been anticipated because the Bible states that man shall have domain over the beasts of the earth.

GENETIC PROFILING

This is a new and rapidly developing science. We all have genes on our chromosomes and these are now being mapped. The use of this information has major ethical problems. For example, cancer of the breast, which is a major problem in the UK. Two genes for breast cancer have been mapped (BRC Al and BRC A2) and it is estimated that 80% of women with these genes will develop breast cancer. What action should be taken? Some pre-menopausal women with these genes have elected to have both breasts removed. One major ethical problem has arisen. Women (and men) when applying for life insurance are asked to declare whether they have had a genetic profile done and, if so, with what result. If the result is positive for any particular disease then life insurance may be rejected or very much weighted in favour of the insurance company. This is quite wrong because insurance implies a risk which affects both sides. A positive test could also affect employment. Employers have no legal right to this information but could insist on a pre-employment medical examination and employment would be subject to a doctor's report. The applicant would have to consent to the examination and the release of the report. If he refused he would not be considered for employment. This is a difficult situation for the Industrial Medical Officer who is employed by the employer. It appears that the Government will allow insurance companies to:

> assess a person's risk of inheriting serious illness. People
> with a genetic tendency to chronic conditions will face

significantly higher premiums for medical, life and travel insurance. (*The Daily Telegraph* 20 March, 2000)

Another ethical problem arises from in vitro fertilisation. If a woman has had a child born with abnormalities or has a family history of congenital disease, she can ask for a genetic profile of an embryo created by artificial insemination and be given a choice whether she wants the embryo implanted or not. The law allows this in cases where there is a family history of genetically determined disease. I entirely agree with this but others would argue that the science of Eugenics is around the corner!

SEXUAL REVOLUTION
This occurred in the 1960's. The skirts became shorter and shorter until they were nothing more than pelmets. Women were liberated and burnt their bras to prove it. 'Make Love Not War' they said and I saw this notice on the back of a lorry: 'Make Love Not War' – See Driver For Details.'

The contraceptive Pill was a major advance in medical science and is now the commonest form of contraception among young people and the most reliable, if taken properly. The Bible tells us that the Wise Virgins put oil in their lamps when they went out at night. Nowadays, the wise virgins are on the Pill. Providing contraceptive advice for a girl under 16 without the consent of her parents is lawful under certain defined conditions. This is an ethical problem but strict confidentiality applies to the girl under 16 if she is deemed to be sufficiently mature and informed. A more difficult ethical problem that I have met is when the under-16 pregnant girl wants an abortion and her mother refuses to sanction it. The legal situation is quite clear. Provided the girl is mature and fully understands what she is requesting, the doctor will find it hard to refuse termination of the pregnancy despite her age and her mother's objections. A doctor's life is not always an easy one but his duty is to act in the best interests of his patient – in this case the underage girl and not her mother.

POST TRAUMATIC STRESS DISORDER

This is a problem which is common to medicine and the law. It is difficult to diagnose and lends itself to abuse. Firemen and ambulance personnel should expect to see 'stressful incidents' as part of their work. The modern trend is for counselling. To me this shows a lack of moral fibre in the affected individual. It is much too easy to 'report sick' and if this is prolonged a diagnosis of post traumatic stress disorder is the new label, sometimes leading to compensation.

Another aspect of the problem which greatly annoys me is that certain civil servants, e.g. policemen, teachers and Social Service personnel, retire on health grounds when faced with disciplinary investigations and may leave the service with an 'ill-health' pension. A House of Commons Home Affairs Committee looked at this problem and, in particular, at the police playing the 'health card'. In an appendix to the report Scotland Yard commented:

> There remains a real concern that officers who are ostensibly mentally strong before their suspension suffer psychiatric illness immediately afterwards and yet so quickly recover following retirement to the extent they are able to function in demanding areas of employment. (*The Daily Telegraph* 1997)

The headline in another paper referring to the same problem read, 'Police quit under cover of sickness, says report.' This is a realistic statement of exactly what sometimes happens and it is a problem the Home Office should investigate. Lord Denning, way back in 1970, said that there is a difference between grief and sorrow, and that a diagnosis of post-traumatic stress disorder could only be made where there is 'some recognised psychiatric illness'. (Hinz v Berry, 1970)

DEATH

Death is inevitable and we should accept it as such. Psalm 90 v 10 states, 'The days of our years are three score years and ten; and if by means of strength they may be fourscore years, yet is their strength labour and sorrow; for it is soon cut off, and we fly away.'

The best place for a golfer to die is on the golf course, but oftentimes the relatives do not accept this as fair comment. Modern medicine and a better environment have given us added years and too often today death is seen as a failure of medical treatment. Death has been medicalised and 'a soulless death in intensive care is the most modern of deaths.' (*British Medical Journal* 2000). It is in the context of intensive care that a Living Will comes into its own. It is my opinion that when death is inevitable and when treatment is futile then treatment should be withdrawn. The law allows this provided it is in the patient's best interests. The patient should be consulted if at all possible. The relatives should also be involved, but they have no legal right to decide an issue such as this. In practice the relatives usually say, 'You won't let him suffer, will you?' This is their basic concern. When a person has had a full and happy life he can look back and accept the fact that one cannot go on forever. There is no cure for birth or death, therefore, one should enjoy the interval in between and be able to justify what 'someone' said, 'Say not in grief – alas he died, but with gratitude – he lived!'

Mark Twain (1835-1910) put it in simpler terms when he said, 'Let us endeavour so to live that when we die even the undertaker will be sorry.'

HOBBIES

It would be wrong to end this book on the subject of death however relevant that is. Everyone should have a hobby, which can be defined as any activity which enables the person to relax, and 're-charge his batteries' by doing something he enjoys and which is different to his routine work. A hobby should be part of every person's life long before retirement, and physical activity in early years would contribute to a longer retirement through improved health.

My main hobby has been gardening. In the house where I live in Aberystwyth we have a small garden which can be very colourful in the summer, and the flowers border a lawn which is ample for the deckchairs in the warm sunshine – when it appears! I have two other gardens, one in Montgomeryshire and one in Llanbadarn. Many years ago I bought a field in my home village of Commins Coch. It is about one acre in size, faces south and as such gets maximum sunshine. Below the field is the river Twymyn and on the other side of the river is my old home Tycerrig and the fields of the farm connected with it.

It was my intention to build a replica of a Welsh Long House on this field. The typical Welsh Long House was usually single story with a central entrance. The cows were housed on the left side and the family lived on right side at a slightly higher level (about 1ft.). Cows generate a lot of heat and they helped keep the house warm. The site in Commins Coch was prepared for this and a septic tank was constructed, also mains water brought to the site and electricity. We had a toilet block and a caravan. I did not proceed with building the house because, as outlined in Chapter 12, I embarked on a new academic course but despite this I spent a lot of time on my 'plot' constructing stone walls, a patio and a barbecue, also digging very deep into the ground to get excellent road making material. I named the proposed building site Swn-y-Nant (Sound of the Stream) because it has two streams running along two borders and these run into the river Twymyn. When I listen to the sound of the water in these streams the poem by Ceiriog comes to mind:

> Nant y mynydd groyw, loyw,
> Yn ymdroelli tua'r pant,
> Rhwng y brwyn yn sisial ganu,
> O na bawn i fel y nant.

Ceiriog (John Ceiriog Hughes, 1832-87) had moved from a rural and mountainous area in North Wales to a totally flat area, Caersws, and this was his way of expressing his *hiraeth,* his longing for the mountains. This is a translation of his poem:

Mountain stream, clear and limpid,
Wandering down towards the valley,
Whispering songs among the rushes,
Oh, that I was as the stream.

(Trans. Kenneth H Jackson, *The Oxford Book of Welsh Verse in English,* Oxford University Press, 1977)

I have planted hundreds and hundreds of daffodils on the plot and these are at their best in a natural environment.

My other garden is in Llanbadarn, a suburb of Aberystwyth, and consists of a building plot, which I bought about 30 years ago. My mother moved from Commins Coch at that time and she had a bungalow built on an adjoining plot. This is a gorgeous site with a small but very productive vegetable garden and lots and lots of flowers.

Of the two gardens, which do I like best? The Llanbadarn garden is nearby and the Commins Coch garden 25 miles away but despite this I am marginally more in favour of the garden and field in Commins Coch because I am on home ground and, to a certain extent, part of the soil of Montgomeryshire. I will finish this narrative by paraphrasing Eifion Wyn in his poem 'Cwm Pennant', first in translation so that I can finish the book in the language of Heaven:

Why, Lord, makest thou Montgomeryshire so beautiful and the life of an old doctor so short?

Pam, Arglwydd, y gwnaethost Sir Drefaldwyn mor dlws,
A bywyd hen feddyg mor fyr?

MEDICAL HUMOUR – AN APPENDIX!

In my introduction to this book I referred to humour in a medical practice and quoted examples of unconscious humour. In this Appendix, I have chosen a few more examples of humour in a medical context, which I hope will amuse the reader.

ACKNOWLEDGEMENTS

The humorous items reproduced in this book were collected over a period of half a century. Publication was not anticipated in the early years with the result that the source of many of the quotations were not recorded and, consequently, not known today. Medical humour owes its prominence in medical literature to three outstanding doctors who not only had a sense of humour but also had mastered the art of communication in print – Dr Michael O'Donnell, Dr David Delvin and Dr Dick Richards. It is also prudent to pay tribute to the medical periodicals which enabled the medical humorists to share their expertise with the medical profession in general and, at the same time, greatly enhance the value and interest of the publications concerned. I refer to *World Medicine, Medical Digest, Medical News, British Journal of Sexual Medicine*, and the triad that have stood the test of time – *Pulse, G.P.*, and *Doctor* – a list which is by no means exhaustive. Newspapers are also a fruitful source of humour and, in particular, the 'Letters to the Editor'. I am indebted to *The Times, The Daily Telegraph, The Sunday Times*, and *The Western Mail* for permission to reproduce items of medical interest collected from these newspapers over the past 50 years. Items from other newspapers and periodicals have been cited whenever possible and in this respect I owe a great debt of gratitude to the

Daily Express, Daily Mail, Daily Mirror, Mail on Sunday, Liverpool Daily Post, Radio Times and *Punch*. As previously stated I have no record of the source of many of the items included in this anthology and I trust and hope that the publishers of the books, periodicals and newspapers concerned will accept my thanks for a blanket permission to reproduce some gems from their publications. *Reader's Digest*, an outstanding publication, has been a rich source of medical humour. I suspect that some of the stories in my collection may have originally appeared in *Reader's Digest* but not acknowledged as such. My apologies, and thanks, to the Editor for my unwitted transgression. Items from the two prestigious medical journals – *The Lancet* and the *British Medical Journal* – also appear in this anthology and there may be instances where due acknowledgement is missing owing to lack of accurate recording in the early years.

The journal *World Medicine* sadly ceased publication about twenty years ago. The author has made every effort to contact copyright owners of copyright information but with negative results. He will be happy to acknowledge copyright ownership in any future editions.

NOTE

The stories in this book are not from my head. All I have done is to collect them over a period of 50 years and assemble them together for the benefit of a wider audience.

It is therefore appropriate that I do not personally profit from this book and it is proposed that any profit will be donated to my favourite charity – Cancer and Leukaemia in Childhood (CLIC).

My first grandchild had cancer at the age of twenty months and, as a family, we will always remember the kindness and support of this particular organisation.

SELECTION OF MEDICAL HUMOUR

'Laughter . . . the most civilised music in the world.'
Sir Peter Ustinov (1921 –) in *Dear Me* 1977

A young man had a perforated appendix and after appendicectomy was discharged home. The practice nurse was asked to visit daily to dress the discharging wound. On her first visit to the house she found a note on the door written by the man's wife (who had gone to work):

'Nurse. Please walk in. My husband is in bed waiting for you.'

AN UNFORTUNATE QUESTION
A patient rang up the doctor in the middle of the night. Wife answers, 'Hello.'

Patient, 'Is that the Doctor's Secretary?'

Two men were discussing death. One said, 'It does not worry me at all. The only problem is that you are so very stiff next day.'

OBVIOUSLY
A patient went to the Chemist with his prescription for sleeping tablets. He read the warning on the label, 'These tablets may make you sleepy.'

From: *Rostrum*, Aug/Sept, 1975

ALL SERVICIES SUPPLIED!

Report in a local paper: 'The three occupants of the vehicle were killed, the first two outright, and the third on arrival in hospital.'

Car Sticker: CANCER CURES SMOKING

'I'd love a second honeymoon – trouble is my Doris would want to go as well.' — Gren

South Wales Echo 6.8.91
Reproduced with permission of Western Mail and Echo Ltd.

Last entry in a patient's medical File: 'Patient had a quiet night. Died at 4.30 am.'

UNFORTUNATELY . . .

A widow, after listening to a good after-dinner speech, said, 'I haven't laughed so much since my husband died.'

And this could well have been factually correct. When completing a death certificate for one of his patients a doctor had entered his own name in the space labelled 'Cause of Death'.

INDUSTRIAL RESEARCH SEEMS TO BE MORE INTERESTING THAN MEDICAL RESEARCH!

Labours in the loo: Lavatory seats should be larger, according to research at the Loughborough University of Technology. Drs Ian McClelland and Joan Ward, sponsored by the Department of Environment, have recently photographed 166 men and women aged between 18 and 81 in a specially constructed experimental lavatory at the Department of Human Sciences at the university. They conclude from their analysis of their measurements (the subjects were naked from the waist down) that the British Standard for lavatory seats is insufficient: for more comfort for most people the interior edge of the seat should be somewhere in the region of two centimetres longer and four centimetres wider. (*Ergonomics*, volume 19, Number 4)

From the *Sunday Times* 29.8.76
Reproduced with the permission of News International Syndication

A CUTTING AND INCISIVE REMARK

During a discussion on breast cancer at a medical conference in San Diego (1981) the question of breast conservation was debated. A lady doctor in the audience got up and said, 'If cancer of the penis was as common as cancer of the breast a better method of treatment than amputation would have been perfected years ago.'

THEM BONES, THEM BONES, THEM . . .

This is a true story attributed to Professor Bernard Knight, the eminent forensic pathologist.

A man in Cardiff moved into a new house and when digging the unkempt garden found a bone and phoned the police. The police called Prof. Knight who declared that it was a human femur. After detailed investigations the story that unfolded gave a simple answer. At one time a medical student was in digs at that house. When he had completed his studies he buried the bones of his study skeleton in the garden.

DRUNK, BUT WHO'S IN CHARGE?

A drunk was going home at 3.00 am. A policeman stopped him and asked, 'Where are you going?'

'To a lecture,' he said.

'Who is going to give you a lecture at this time of the night?' asked the policeman.

'My wife,' was the reply.

CAN WE HAVE – ER– COPYING?

In the early days of the photocopying machine the following notice was attached to the medical office machine in Spokane in Washington:

'No-one shall use the Secretary's reproduction equipment without her express permission.'

BUT WHAT ABOUT THE PRACTICAL LESSONS?

A doctor was asked what he thought of sex education in schools. 'A good idea for children provided they do not have any home-work,' he replied.

THE COUNTER REFORMATION

A small town in Wales had one notorious prostitute. One of the local ministers decided that he would reform her and thought that he had succeeded. Many months later he met her on the street and said, 'Hello, Mary, how are you? I was thinking about you last night.'

'Well, Mr Davies, bach,' she said. 'Why didn't you phone?'

TRIBUTE TO A SUPER DOCTOR

'As a pioneer and professional man Dr Bancky was out in front. Fifty nine years he practised medicine, being responsible for most of the babies born in the community.'

BELTS AND BRACES

A doctor's regular practice was to prescribe the contraceptive pill for six months at a time. One woman returned after three months for a repeat prescription. The doctor pointed out that he had given her enough for six months and asked, 'Do you take one every morning as I explained to you?'

'Yes,' she said, 'but to be on the safe side I give one to my husband as well.'

WOULD THAT BE DAI OR DIE?

Coal mining was, at one time, one of the major industries in Wales and this brought in its wake the disease know as pneumoconiosis, known locally as 'the dust'. The disease was difficult to diagnose in its early stages and compensation was not available unless 'The Board' was satisfied that the patient had the disease.

A young man had worked in the pits for about six months and had to leave because of idiopathic shortness of breath. He visited his doctor and said that he was sure that he had 'the dust'. The doctor examined his chest and said that there was no evidence of this.

Three months later he was back again saying that he was sure he had the disease and demanding to have an X-ray. This was done and was normal.

A few months later he was back again and repeating his conviction that he had the 'dust' and that he should have 'compo'. He demanded to see the Chest Physician. This was duly arranged and, the report was negative and a repeat chest X-ray was normal. Six months later he was back again and said to the doctor, 'I am certain that I have pneumoconiosis despite what you all say. I demand a post-mortem.'

GRANN-E-MAIL

A pupil in school was asked, 'What is the Internet?'

'The Internet is what grandma wears over her curlers when she goes to bed at night,' was the quick reply.

COMMUNICATE!

It is good practice to ask patients how they got on when in hospital. Invariably they are satisfied but with one reservation, 'The doctors are good, the nurses are very nice, but they don't tell you anything.' Communication is sadly at fault in the doctor/patient relationship, and one can well believe the story of a patient who used the portable bedside telephone to ask the ward sister how she was that day . . .

A CALMER KARMA?

The grandmother had died and the two young grandchildren were confused. One said to the other, 'Where's Grandma gone?'

'Grandma's gone to Heaven.'

'What has she gone to Heaven for?' was the next question.

'She's gone to Heaven to be recycled,' was the mature reply.

THE OFFICIAL POSITION?

A family planning clinic was held between 7.00 and 9.00 pm in the local hospital. This meant that porters had to be paid overtime to lock the front door after the clinic. On the next clinic day patients saw this notice outside the hospital front door:

'For Family Planning please use the back entrance.'

(Original version appeared in *Guy's Hospital Gazette*)

'The doctor told me to avoid fat, so I'm leaving you.'
Medical Digest Feb. 1973

COULD THIS HAPPEN TODAY?

'I've been to see my doctor twice in the past 18 months. His surgery is apart from his group practice premises, and he never removes his hat or coat, which makes me feel as if I am keeping him from an important appointment. He writes out the prescription while I'm telling him what's wrong with me, and he never removes his cigarette from his mouth when he speaks.'

Letter from a Mrs J.S., Stockport, Cheshire. Circa 1969

Headline in a local paper: MAN FOUND DEAD IN CEMETERY.

WORLDS APART . . .

Communication is very important in all walks of life and particularly so in medical practice when doctor and patient must be on the same wavelength. An Indian gentleman visited his doctor with the complaint that he was very worried because he could not have sex with his wife. The doctor explained briefly the possible causes of this unfortunate complaint and then asked his patient, 'Into which category do you think you belong?'

'My problem, doctor, is very simple. I am here in Aberystwyth and my wife is in India,' was his quick reply.

BE YE NOT AFRAID

A consultant surgeon hired a maid. When she arrived he took her to her bedroom. Next morning she said she was leaving. Asked why she said, 'It's that picture above my bed. The picture is nice but the writing on it alarms me'

This puzzled the surgeon because he had not taken any notice of the picture. He asked the girl what was the writing she objected to.

'Therefore be ye prepared for thou knowest not when thy Master cometh,' was her reply.

PRECISELY HOW VAGUE?

Medicine is an art and a science. This is an example of the art of medicine. A patient came to the doctor with vague symptoms which did not add up to anything. After examination the doctor said, 'There's a lot of this around.'

The patient was quite happy with that diagnosis.

PEE-TOTAL!

Nocturia is a common complaint, as men get older. One man had a remedy! An Irishman bought five bottles of Guinness on his way home from work. He poured three of them down the toilet. His wife was puzzled. 'Why did you do that?' she asked.

'That will save me getting up at night,' he replied.

Derek Steinberg
World Medicine 8.2.78

TAX INSPECTORS AVERT YOUR EYES!

A GP took a consulting surgeon on a private domiciliary visit to a farmer in rural Wales. After the consultation the farmer asked the surgeon about his fee and was told the amount. He took out his cheque book and filled in the cheque counterfoil. The surgeon, looking over his shoulder, said, 'Excuse me. That is not my name.'

'Don't worry Mr Griffiths bach, I'm putting you down as a load of manure.'

I MEAN . . . TO SAY

A Bank Manager told a Cardiganshire man that his account was overdrawn.

'Can't be,' said the Cardi, 'I still have ten cheques in my cheque book.'

THE MARRIAGE AFFLICTION?

A lady arrived at a surgery with her nine kids for a blood pressure examination. When the GP, during the consultation, mentioned her husband, she became rather embarrassed.

'Well . . . he isn't actually my husband, though we've lived together for 25 years.'

'Oh? How is that?'

'Well, when I was young my doctor found I had diabetes and said I ought never to get married.'

GP December 1972 (Reproduced with the permission of the Deputy Editor)

THE NEW BUREAUCRACY
ARGYLL AND CLYDE HEALTH BOARD AREA LAUNDRY

Subject: *Common User Item – Knickers*

At the recent Laundry Users Committee meeting held on Monday, 3rd September 1979 the above named subject was discussed. It was agreed that due to the seemingly *(sic)* shortage of the item in question, an inventory be taken at 0800 hours on Monday, 8th October, 1979. This project will of course require the full co-operation of nursing and ancillary staff. Any additional information required please contact Mr J. Gill at the Area Laundry.

John McNeil, Area Laundry Manager

World Medicine 3.11.79

BEDPAN STEERING COMMITTEE

A meeting of the Bedpan Steering Committee will be held on Monday, 12th March, 1979 at 10.30 a.m. in the Conference Room, Medical Centre.

— Memo from Principal Assistant Administrator,
Hounslow Health District
World Medicine 7.4.79

GREENWICH & BEXLEY AREA HEALTH AUTHORITY
BEXLEY HEALTH DISTRICT

Date: 15th March 1976

From: Hospital Administrator
To: All Heads of Departments
Subject or Reference: Toilet Paper JJ/GEE

Would you please note that the soft paper
toilet rolls are provided only for the use of
patients and not staff. It would appear that
in recent months the staff have been using the
soft toilet rolls for one reason or another.
If, to your knowledge, this practice exists in
your department, would you please take the
appropriate steps to stop it.

World Medicine 7.4.76

A FINE LINE . . .

A lady attended the local hospital for a check-up. The doctor
examined her abdomen and said to the attending nurse, 'Look at
this. What a neat caesarean scar.'

The nurse did not reply but the patient said that it was the
impression left by the seam of her tights.

A man consulted his GP. After the examination and advice he said
to the doctor, 'I want a second opinion.'

'Certainly,' said the doctor. 'Come back to see me tomorrow.'

WELSH EXPERIENCES

I am a general practitioner aged 70, and am retiring this year. I was
interested in the issue of *GP* of July 6 as when I came out of the

RAMC I worked in Tredegar in the Workmen's Medical Aid Society started by Nye Bevan, and lived in Dr Cronin's house. I would like to quote one experience I had. A patient came up to see me one Sunday morning and asked for a 'paper', meaning a certificate. When I said I would like to examine him, he immediately retorted 'I have not come for a bloody examination but for my paper.' I persuaded him to let me examine him and afterwards he said, 'Duw, Duw, I have been coming for the last 20 years and no bugger has ever bloody done that to me. Thank you very much Doctor.'

Dr A.V. Griffiths, The Parade, Pagham

Part of a letter published in *GP* 7.9.73
Reproduced with the permission of the Deputy Editor

Yes — it does happen!

A woman who did not know she was pregnant gave birth to an eight-pound baby boy six hours after being treated by a doctor for lumbago.

News Report. Quoted in *Pulse* 1973
Reproduced with the permission of the editor

What a load of scruples!

A young wife consulted her doctor complaining (as they often do) about her husband. She said that he was a very fussy man — he would not sleep with her because she was a married woman.

Cartoon in a San Diego newspaper, October 1981
Wife: The kids never come when I call them
Husband: So, maybe they'll grow up to be doctors.

'Twins! Oh, how wonderful – one for each father!'
Pulse 4.11.72 (Reproduced with permission of the Editor)

A SIREN?

'Sister Shirley competes for the Daily Express Nurse of the Year title this month. She said that the Hospital's ambulance men had entered her without her knowing.'

Lyford and Redbridge Pictorial. Quoted in *World Medicine*

IT'S AN IDEA . . .

Sex education starts early these days. Children were asked about 'making a baby'. A four-year-old girl had some idea that fathers are connected with the birth process. She said, 'The daddy puts his hand in his tummy and puts the seed on the bottom of the mummy.'

The Sunday Times 18.5.75

Comment: It could be said that the four year old was describing in vitro fertilisation, long before it became part of modern medicine.

Verse needs treatment

In 1981 *World Medicine* ran a Medical Limerick Competition. Among the entries which had 'an honourable mention' was the following entry from Dr Ian Pitter.

> A G.P.'s pert, pretty young daughter
> Gave her father a sample of water,
> Saying 'Dad, here's some wee;
> Would you test it for me?
> As I've not been as good as I oughter.'

World Medicine 22.8.81 'Dr Jekyll'.

The Changing Pattern of Medical Care in the Community

Dr Phillips used the occasion of his retirement to offer some robust thoughts on the state of general practice.

'I think young GPs have it much easier today. They move into ready-made group practices.

'In former days doctors wore white coats over dark suits, polished their nails, had excellent bedside manners and took pride in being professional to their fingertips.

'A doctor's income equated with his expertise, not to numbers. They had to work hard to increase their numbers and did not have a ready-made practice to enter.

'Now they talk about Marbella and the replacement car. The list is too great and patients are seen as statistics.'

Dr Phillips added: 'Respect is diminishing. Before 1948 when a doctor called at a house the room was tidy, there was clean bed linen, a wash basin, towel and soap at hand, the dog chained up, the pottie under the bed and the children all seated with their hands folded.

'Now the dog greets you first, the radio is blaring away, the husband is smoking and watching TV, the mother is finishing her washing in another room, there is no chair to sit on, no wash basin, the pottie is still full and children are running about the room.

'The diagnosis has been made by a neighbour and all that is wanted is some antibiotics or a referral to hospital.'

Dr Jack Phillips, Newcastle, on his retirement at the age of 81.

Pulse 8.12.84 (Reproduced with the permission of the Editor)

COULD BE TRUE!

Husband to wife: 'I'm all right. My doctor gave me a brain scan and found nothing.'

P-FREE AT NEW CAR PARK TILL MONDAY

Jersey Evening Post, June 1, 1972 (Reproduced with the permission of the Editor)

PATIENT PEDANTRY!

The doctor told his patient not to drink any more alcohol. At a follow-up consultation the patient said, 'I'm not drinking any more, and I'm not drinking any less.'

AN UNUSUAL CAUSE OF A FRACTURE

Seam stress: Petrol station attendant Sue Parkin of Sheffield broke a finger as she tried to take off a pair of tight jeans.

Daily Mail 22.9.86 (Reproduced with the permission of *The Daily Mail*)

DOCTORS BEWARE!

'I fear the man who drinks water. As he remembers this morning what the rest of us said last night.'

Ancient Greek Anthology

CORRELATION?

As the pay strike by Israel's salaried doctors entered its third week, officials reported that the country's death rate had dropped by nearly a third. In Haifa, undertakers said that funerals were down by a half.

The Sunday Times 1.7.73
Reproduced with the permission of News International Syndication

PROTOCOLS NEED CAREFUL WORDING

'When tube feeding, the nurse should first pass water down the tube.'

Guys Hospital Gazette c 1975

TELL ME WHAT I MEAN, PLEASE!

A few examples of letters received by the Ministry of Social Security in Edinburgh, which dealt with Public Welfare. (c 1963):

'I am glad to say my husband died yesterday. I will be glad if you will get me a pension.'

'In accordance with your instructions I gave birth to twins in the enclosed envelope.'

'Milk is needed for the baby. Father is unable to supply it. Re your dental enquiry, the teeth at the top are alright but the ones in my bottom are hurting terrible.'

'I want money as quick as possible. I have been in bed with a doctor for a week and he doesn't seem to be doing any good. If things don't improve I will have to get another doctor.'

A GOLDEN RULE FOR ALL DOCTORS

Never discuss anything with a patient (female in this example) until she is dressed and sitting comfortably in a chair.

For example: Report on Maternity Care in London '... difficult to demand information when you're on a couch with your knickers off, and when doctors use such big words.'

Susannah Clapp, *Sunday Times* Radio Critic. 22.10.78
Reproduced with the permission of News International Syndication

Doctor to a curvaceous young lady: 'No, it's not wind, Miss Chapman. Guess again.'

Keep your husband out of draughts,
keep the windows, doors and your mouth shut.
Rostrum No 59, 1976

THE CAMP PISSICIAN . . .

At a military transit camp in Takoradi, the Gold Coast, during the war the following notice was displayed in every room:

'No water must be drunk in this camp unless it has been passed by the Medical Officer.'

FEEL THE KNEED. . .

A man complained of pain in his right knee. After examination, the doctor told him that it was old age. The man said, 'That can't be right. The left knee is the same age and that is not painful.'

AN EXCELLENT IDEA!

Headline in *British Medical Journal* 1.3.97: BRINGING NURSES AND DOCTORS CLOSER TOGETHER.

FERROUS ENOUGH!

A patient was told by the doctor to stop the iron medicine for the time being

'Will it keep?' she asked.

'Certainly it will,' said the doctor.

'I am so glad,' she said. 'I was afraid it might go rusty.'

FOR SALE

Half skeleton: Only one previous owner, £30.
Tel: Welwyn Garden City 28111.'

'On Call', *World Medicine* 19.10.77

WHAT THE PAPERS SAY

'Mothercare toilet seat and stool, £3 ono'

'On Call', *World Medicine* 24.8.77

Wedding dress for sale. Never used.
Bride put on weight. Price £15.

Advert in local paper, 1965

The complete outfit:
'Model wedding dress with train, long veil,
attached to Dutch cap. £25.'

Small advert in *Andover Advertiser,* quoted in *World Medicine* 24.2.79

Advert for hospital domestic staff:
'Cleaner Wanted for male areas.'

A private patient in a hospital bed received a card from BUPA: 'Wishing you a speedy recovery.'

LOOK IT UP!

Men who hope ultimately to be domiciled in Heaven should take adequate precautions on earth: 'He that is wounded in the stones or has his privy member cut off shall not enter into the congregation of the Lord.' Deuteronomy 23.1

A group of men who had had a vasectomy arranged a vasectomy party. The children in the house were wondering what it was all about. They were told:

1 'Don't ask questions.'
2 'You're lucky to be here at all.'

Punch December 1973 (Reproduced with permission).

SIMPLE QUESTIONS – INSTANT DIAGNOSIS

'Have you had this before?'
'Yes doctor.'
'Well, you've got it again.'

MANY DOCTORS COULD SAY THE SAME THING

My friend, who is expecting twins took her small daughter to see the ultra sound scan. After studying the monitor for a few minutes, her daughter whispered, 'They need a new telly.'

Denice Gill, Liverpool.

Daily Mail 30.9.95 (Reproduced with permission).

WE ALL MAKE MISTAKES...

'My doctor diagnosed my complaint as indigestion. Now indigestion is five years old and starts school in September.'

MOO-SIC WHILE YOU MILK

A leading agriculture research establishment in Mid Wales researched the effects of music in the cowshed during milking, based on the war time 'Music While you Work' which increased production in armament factories. There was a slight increase in milk yield but this was not really significant.

The next step was to install television in the cowshed. There was no response until one morning there was a considerable increase in milk yield. The research workers were most anxious to know what was shown on the TV screen the night before. They discovered that there was only one item televised all evening: 'Normal service will be resumed as soon as possible.'

ONCE UPON A TIME!

A long forgotten letter to *Pulse*.

Doctors are still reaping the benefit from the change in women's fashions. Tights replaced combinations. What a relief!

'Carry on wearing the mini, girls,' pleads Dr John Hughes of Aberystwyth, in the medical newspaper *Pulse*. He claims it makes his work easier.

'Access to the legs and abdomen has been easy and very much

quicker. The recent no-bra era has made things even easier,' he says.

'Heaven forbid that we return to the days of obstructive corsetry, clumsy ironmongery, long-legged knickers, flowing dresses and long leather boots.'

Thanks for the tonic, doc.

Sex and Common Sense

A BBC programme debated the problem of sex education with parents, teachers, adolescents and educationalists. But what – and how – do children themselves know about sex? Harold Williamson talks to some of the youngsters:

Françoise Evans (5 years):

'My mummy didn't know I was going to be born. She didn't know if I was going to be one or two or three babies. Or a boy or a girl.

It was funny and I just came. Mummy got an injection in her bottom and I just came out. It was in hospital and the doctor put me in her arms. I can remember. Then we all came home.

My daddy didn't have anything to do with it. He works. You have to feed the baby. You know those things that stick out from a woman in front. You put one in the baby's mouth and it sucks all the milk out.

Nobody told me. I just learned myself. I just thought about it and pictures came in my head. Then I knew. Sometimes I don't see pictures. Sometimes I do.

Some people think you can go to a shop and buy babies, but that's not true. But there's no way to know if a baby is going to be nice or nasty. I don't think that's fair.'

Anna Beaver (10 years):

'I have heard of ladies having babies without being married but, myself, I think you have to be married. It would not be easy if the mother was not married. The baby would not have a father and the mother would not have anybody to help her at all. It would be best to get married first.

It starts after an egg and after months and days of waiting. My mummy told me and it is a long time ago. I can't remember when I didn't know it. She also gave me a book with how all your body works. Your ears and heart and everything.

I think the father has something to do with it. Mummy has told me about it but I don't think I really understand it yet. In the little bags between his legs there are eggs, which are small, and I think they help to make a baby as well but I don't think I know much more.

One girl said babies came out of mummy's mouth but they don't. From the stomach.'

Radio Times June 1971 Issue 26 June – 2 July 1971.

Reproduced with permission

ADVERT IN *RIKERSERVICE* 22.10.76

Wanted: Doctor's bag with drawers in good condition. Please write 17 Woodbourne Rd. Brooklands, Manchester.

Mother to daughter as she goes out for the evening:

'Remember, dear, just because you've reached the age of consent, it doesn't mean you have to.'

Daily Mirror 7.8.75 (Reproduced with permission).

HOW A–PEE–LING!

I would have taken my water tablets but I did not want to go over my doctor's head.

Note from patient. *World Medicine* 3.5.80

First the good news. His temperature has gone down.

Punch 30.1.74 (Reproduced with permission)

The basic truth before the Human Fertilisation and Embryology Act:

Q. 'What causes a woman to have twins or triplets?'

A. 'The same thing.'

INTERNAL MEMO IN A GLASGOW HOSPITAL

To: Staff

Both my consultant colleagues and myself are anxious to increase the number of post-mortems performed. We should be grateful for your co-operation.

Quoted in *World Medicine* 22.9.76

Nurses have to help her on and off a commode. The nursing home's proprietor comments, 'I don't know what happens to these poor old lasses who fall between two stools.'

The Observer, quoted in *World Medicine*

DOCTORS MUST HAVE A VOCATION — SURELY?
'Who but they can enjoy holding up a jar of mucus, faeces or urine to the light and regarding it with the interest and satisfaction more usually displayed by connoisseurs of rare wine?'

Mary Bourne. *Pulse* 2.4.77 (Reproduced with permission)

I GIVE UP!
Professor Seaborne Davies, the eminent lawyer, told this story about himself. When he retired from his post as Professor of Law at Liverpool University he was given the title of Emeritus Professor in accordance with custom. This duly appeared as a news item in his local paper. At the next Council meeting one of the Councillors addressed the Mayor and said, 'Mr Mayor, one of the sons of this town has had a great honour. He has been made an Emeritus Professor. I propose that we write to congratulate him and in my opinion he should have had this honour years ago.'

A rather disturbing notice seen
outside a hospital in Harrogate . . .
'BEWARE! GUARD DOGS OPERATING!'
Sent to a newspaper by Keith Machie, Harrogate, Yorks. (Age 13)

KILL OR CURE . . .
A depressed man attempted suicide by walking into the sea. After taking a few paces in the water he abandoned the mission.
'Why did you give up?' asked the psychiatrist.
'The water was too cold,' was the reply.

Another depressed man contemplated suicide, bought 100 aspirins, took two, and felt better.

Conception Vol 1 No 6

Doctors have to be careful what they say to patients:
Patient to Doctor: 'I'm afraid I'm at death's door.'
Doctor to Patient: 'Don't you worry, we'll pull you through.'

World Medicine, 17.7.74

Doctor, after examining a man, said to his wife:
   'I don't like the look of your husband.'
   'Neither do I,' she replied. 'But he's good to our children.'

OH, BROTHER! WHAT A MISPRINT!
Birth Announcement: 'To Gwenfron and Ifor at Bronglais Hospital, Aberystwyth, a git of a brother for Blodwen.'

THE NEW BUREAUCRACY – DEAD RECKONING!
From Minute 146 of the Medical Executive Committee Essex AHA, Colchester District . . .
Deceased Patients' Appointments: Members hoped that some solution would be found to the problem of communications sent out by hospitals to patients after their death.

World Medicine 2.6.79

A-PAULING! A LITERARY DRUNK
Dr Paul, a GP in Aberystwyth, was getting on in years. He lived in the main street and had his nameplate outside his residence. One night a drunk rang the bell. The doctor appeared at the bedroom window:

'Are you Dr Paul?' asked the drunk.

'Yes,' replied the doctor.

'Are you the real Paul?' asked the drunk.

'Yes, of course,' said the doctor. 'What do you want?'

'One thing I always wanted to know. Did you get a reply to your letter to the Corinthians?'

Y DIWEDD – THE END – FINIS